A MAN'S GUIDE TO THE

SPIRITUAL
DISCIPLINES

A MAN'S GUIDE TO THE
SPIRITUAL DISCIPLINES

12 HABITS TO STRENGTHEN YOUR WALK WITH CHRIST

PATRICK MORLEY

MOODY PUBLISHERS

CHICAGO

Scripture quotations marked NIV are taken from the *Holy Bible, New International Version*®. NIV®. Copyright © 1973, 1978, 1984 by International Bible Society. Used by permission of Zondervan . All rights reserved.

Scripture quotations marked KJV are taken from the King James Version.

Published in association with the literary agency of Wolgemuth & Associates, Inc.

Cover Design: Brand Navigation, LLC DeAnna Pierce, Bill Chiaravalle,
        www.brandnavigation.com
Cover Images: Corbis, Digital Stock, Getty Images
Interior Design: Ragont Design
Editor: Jim Vincent

Library of Congress Cataloging-in-Publication Data

Morley, Patrick M.
    A man's guide to the spiritual disciplines : 12 habits to strengthen your walk with Christ /
by Patrick Morley.
    p. cm.
    Includes bibliographical references.
    ISBN-13: 978-0-8024-7551-0
    1. Men—Religious life. 2. Men—Conduct of life. I. Title.

BV4528.2.M675 2007
248.8'42—dc22

                                                        2006032851

                        ISBN: 0-8024-7551-5
                        ISBN-13: 978-0-8024-7551-0

We hope you enjoy this book from Moody Publishers. Our goal is to provide high-quality, thought-provoking books and products that connect truth to your real needs and challenges. For more information on other books and products written and produced from a biblical perspective, go to www.moodypublishers.com or write to:

Moody Publishers
820 N. LaSalle Boulevard
Chicago, IL 60610

3 5 7 9 10 8 6 4 2

Printed in the United States of America

To Jim Seibert,

My friend and co-laborer for two decades.
Your servant heart and passion for Christ
inspire me to be a better man.
Thanks for making me laugh.

CONTENTS

ACKNOWLEDGMENTS

A book is never really the work of one person. This book began as a twelve- message series at The Man in the Mirror Bible Study entitled "Spiritual Disciplines for the Man in the Mirror." My deepest appreciation goes to Daphne Mayer for getting the messages transcribed, and for tracking down hundreds of research details and keeping other boats floating while I wrote. Special thanks to Ruth Ford for transforming the transcriptions from the spoken word to a written style.

Thank you, Robert Wolgemuth, my literary agent and friend. You launched my writing career and, as always, found the right home for this book.

Gratitude must be offered to Moody Publishers for accepting me as a men's author. Everyone on the Moody team has gone above and beyond to make me feel welcome and to develop the best possible book. Special thanks to Greg Thornton, as well as Steve Lyon, Dave DeWit, John Hinkley, Paul Santhouse, and my editor, Jim Vincent.

As always, my wife, Patsy, acted as my sounding board, offering both encouragement and wisdom. The staff and directors at Man in the Mirror graciously allowed me to focus on writing. I thank you for executing so well that I was free to pursue this book.

And a special thank-you to the men at The Man in the Mirror Bible Study, where I had the privilege of working out these ideas. Thanks, guys.

A GUIDE TO GROUP DISCUSSION

Any man interested in starting a group to discuss *A Man's Guide to the Spiritual Disciplines* can successfully do so and lead a lively discussion. Each chapter contains helpful discussion questions. But before you form a discussion group, consider the following guidelines, which can help any discussion leader.

Starting a Group

Share a copy of this book with the men with whom you want to meet. Alternatively, copy the table of contents and the discussion questions from the end of a few chapters. Ask them if they would like to be in a discussion group that would read and discuss the material. This can be a group from your work, church, neighborhood, recreation, or a combination. Invite anyone you would like. The optimum size for the group would be four to six men.

When You First Meet

The first week together, distribute a copy of the book to each member and a schedule of your upcoming meetings. Assign the first chapter as next week's reading assignment and ask them to be prepared to answer the questions at the end of the chapter.

Then go around the room and ask each man to share with the group where he is on his spiritual pilgrimage. This is a great icebreaker, and the men will be encouraged to hear one another's stories. Be sure to point out that there are no wrong answers to this question. Some may just be starting on their pilgrimage; others may be well down the road. Close with a prayer. Always adjourn exactly when you said you would.

Typical Week

Begin with an icebreaker question. As an alternative, you may ask a different man each week to give a maximum five-minute personal testimony of how he became a Christian. Here is a good schedule for a one-hour meeting:

- Ten minutes Icebreaker/Fellowship

- Forty minutes Discussion Questions

- Ten minutes Group Prayer

- End promptly at the scheduled time

For a ninety-minute meeting, add twenty minutes to the discussion, and five minutes to the fellowship and prayer times.

Leading the Discussion

The best groups are facilitated by shepherds, not teachers. Don't feel as if you have to have all the answers. Rather, your role is to encourage each man to share his thoughts. Try to make sure everyone in the group gets some "air time." If someone dominates the time, privately ask them to help you draw out the more reserved members of the group. And remember, it's more important to talk about "real" things than it is to answer every single question.

Experience

You don't have to be an experienced Bible teacher to lead a discussion. If someone asks a question beyond your scope, simply say so and move on.

The Next Step

You have created momentum with the men in your group. Don't finish the study without capturing this momentum. After the fifth or sixth week, begin to let men know your next steps and how they can stay involved. If you will not continue as a group, make sure you take the men to an alternative opportunity (another group, class at your church, etc.) and help them make the transition. Your role is not complete until your men have successfully taken these next steps.

For more information on leading men and additional men's resources, visit www.maninthemirror.org where you will find dozens of leadership training and small-group materials in addition to over five hundred free resources.

AN INTRODUCTION TO THE SPIRITUAL DISCIPLINES

A man said, half jokingly, "Do me a favor. Tell me how to be good. I already know how bad I am." That sentiment captures the intent of this book and the purpose of the spiritual disciplines.

Unfortunately, many men—men who really do want to be good—end up living in a rut. For example, various surveys show that for every ten men in church:

- Nine will watch at least one of their kids walk away from church.
- Eight do not find their jobs satisfying.
- Six pay only the monthly minimum on their credit card balances.
- Five have a major problem with pornography.
- Four will get divorced (affecting one million children per year).
- Only one will have a biblical worldview.
- All ten struggle to balance work and family.[1]

What the Spiritual Disciplines Are and Are Not

Spiritual disciplines are the regular practices men cultivate when they want a closer walk with Christ. The spiritual disciplines can help us break a cycle or get out of a rut. Disciplines are the spiritual habits by which we cultivate a deeper relationship with the Lord of heaven and earth. We perform the disciplines because we want to please God, to lead peaceable lives, to be godly husbands, to raise godly children, and to be men of God.

An athlete who lifts weights as part of a training regimen probably doesn't lift just because he loves pumping iron. He probably wants to improve his strength and endurance (and possibly his appearance). Similarly, disciplines are not ends in themselves—they are means to an end.

To the man who says, "Tell me how to be good," I have a simple yet sober answer: Nothing you do will ever make you good enough for God to love you. Instead, He loves you because He made you, and because Christ died for your sins.

Therefore, spiritual disciplines do nothing to improve your record with God. We don't perform the disciplines to make God happy (or avoid His wrath), or to earn favor or merit with God. All the merit we need, we already have in Christ. We place our trust in God—not in the disciplines.

Nevertheless, disciplines demonstrate to God how serious we are about following Him, and they also help us see how serious we are as well. When all is said and done, spiritual disciplines are the designated means for us to grow in this relationship that we have with Jesus. God is always speaking, so if we don't hear Him, it's not because He has suddenly gone silent. It is more likely that we aren't listening—or perhaps don't know how to listen.

Four Ways That God Communicates

Hearing God is simple but not easy. If it was easy, wouldn't more men be doing it? Since God does not speak in our day through burning bushes or pillars of fire, how does God speak to men today? Every day God is revealing Himself four ways:

- through His *works*

- through His *Word*

- through the *"whisper"* of the Holy Spirit

- through the *witness* of believers

Here is a preview of the twelve disciplines we will be studying built around these four ways that God communicates with mankind.

First, *God communicates through His works.* God speaks to us through His works in creation. "The heavens declare the glory of God; the skies proclaim the work of his hands" (Psalm 19:1). For now, we'll just note that theologians call this *general revelation.* This communication is available to all people all over the world. This will be the subject of chapter 1, "A Man and Creation."

Second, *God communicates through His Word.* God also speaks to us through His Scriptures. Psalm 19:7 says, "The law of the LORD is perfect, reviving the soul." Theologians call this *special revelation.* This will be the subject of chapter 2, "A Man and the Bible."

Third, *God communicates through the "whisper" of the Holy Spirit.* Picture a cube of space in front of you, twelve inches on all sides. Within that one-foot cube of space are all of today's news, radio programming, cell phone conversations, and much more. But in order to hear any of it, you have to be on the right frequency. In the same way, the voice of the Spirit is also right there in front of us in that one-foot cube, but we won't hear Him unless we tune in to the right frequency. In chapters 3–9 (part 3) we will explore several ways we can tune in to what the Spirit has to say on the following topics:

- a man and prayer

- a man and worship

- a man and the Sabbath

- a man and fellowship

- a man and counsel

- a man and fasting

- a man and spiritual warfare

Fourth, *God communicates through the witness of believers.* Finally, God speaks to us (and the lost) through the witness of fellow believers. The first nine disciplines are mainly for us. In the final three chapters (part 4), we will explore the disciplines that mainly help others and help us express neighbor-love:

- a man and stewardship

- a man and service

- a man and evangelism

When I drive my car on short trips around Florida, I often listen to my favorite radio station for as long as I can. But once I'm out of range, the voices fade and I get the whirrrrrr of static. Or I hear another voice from a competing station bleeding onto the same frequency. And then I lose the signal altogether. But just because I've put myself out of range doesn't mean the radio station quits broadcasting the signal.

Similarly, God is always broadcasting through His works, Word, whisper, and witness. We just have to put ourselves within range. I hope this book will help you draw closer to God and clearly hear His voice.

Additional Resources

Celebration of Discipline, by Richard Foster
Disciplines of a Godly Man, by Kent Hughes
The Spirit of the Disciplines, by Dallas Willard
Spiritual Disciplines for the Christian Life, by Donald Whitney

PART ONE

DISCIPLINE RELATED TO THE WORKS OF GOD

A MAN AND CREATION

PREVIEW

In this chapter we will examine what God says about His creation. We'll:

- See how nature reveals God's character.
- Learn why it's important to cultivate an attitude of enjoying God's creation.
- Consider positive ways to begin incorporating this discipline into daily life.

Let's begin this chapter with a brief pop quiz to test your creation IQ.

1. Circle the answer that best reflects how you regard creation. Creation is:

Good   **Evil**   **Neutral**

2. Which of the following answers best describes the relationship between creation (nature, the universe) and God?

a. Nature hints of God.

b. Nature reveals God.

c. Nature conceals God.

d. Nature tarnishes God.

Let's explore how the Bible answers these two questions.

The Bible on Nature

When C. S. Lewis was an atheist, he explained why he didn't believe in God. He wrote,

> Look at the universe we live in. By far the greatest part of it consists of empty space, completely dark and unimaginably cold. . . . It is improbable that any planet except the Earth sustains life. And Earth herself existed without life for millions of years and may exist without life for millions more when life has left her. And what is it like while it lasts? It is so arranged that all the forms of it can live only by preying upon one another. . . . In the most complex of all the creatures, Man, yet another quality appears, which we call reason. . . . It enables men by a hundred ingenious contrivances to inflict a great deal more pain than they otherwise could have done on one another and on the irrational creatures. This power they have exploited to the full. Their history is largely a record of crime, war, disease, and terror, with just sufficient happiness interposed to give them, while it lasts, an agonized apprehension of losing it, and, when it is lost, the poignant misery of remembering. . . .
>
> There was one question which I never dreamed of raising. . . . If the universe is so bad, or even half so bad, how on earth did human beings ever come to attribute it to the activity of a wise and good Creator? Men are fools, perhaps; but hardly so foolish as that.[1]

So is creation good, evil, or neutral? Author Leonard Sweet helps us uncover the answer in his book *Soul Tsunami,* in which he describes his family buying their first television set. His mother was a traveling evangelist, and their church was quite legalistic. The Sweet family bought the set when TVs first became available. One night there came a knock on the door. The pastor had dropped by the house to visit, and the TV happened to be on.

The pastor peered in and said, "So it's true. You have bought the devil's blinking box." Leonard's mother argued that matter is not evil—it's what people do with matter that makes it evil. Still, the Sweet family was put out of the church for having the "devil's blinking box."

Mrs. Sweet was right. Matter itself is not evil. *Nothing* in God's creation is evil—not thunder, lightning, storms, movies, or television signals. And yet, because of the fall, thunder can scare your children, lightning can hit your home and start a fire, storm winds can split a tree that then crashes into your living room, movies can debase human beings made in God's image, and television can bring profanity to your ears and lust to your eyes.

Nevertheless, the Bible says, "The whole earth is full of his *glory*" (Isaiah 6:3, emphasis added). Now, this used to really bother me, because when we look around we see a lot of *evil*. We also see a third force at work in the world: *futility*, or that which simply doesn't matter. I wondered, *How could the earth be full of God's glory when there is so much evil and futility?*

Then one day, while studying glucose, I was struck with an analogy. Glucose is a three-part compound: $C_6 H_{12} O_6$—six parts carbon, twelve parts hydrogen, six parts oxygen. So glucose is full of oxygen, but not only oxygen; it is also full of carbon and hydrogen. In the same way, the earth really is full of God's glory, despite the fact that it is also full of evil and futility.

The Bible also says, "For everything God created is good" (1 Timothy 4:4). Colossians 1:16 goes even further,

> For by [Jesus] all things were created: things in heaven and on earth,
> visible and invisible, whether thrones or powers or rulers or authorities;
> all things were created by him and for him.

So the bottom line in Scripture is this: (1) God made everything. (2) Everything God made is good. Therefore, (3) everything is intrinsically good. That implies that nature has meaning and value. This is not to say that nature is incorruptible. Because of the fall we have to explain the stench of polluted rivers, belching smokestacks, and natural disasters. What the Bible does mean, however, is that apart from sin, nature is good. According to his wife, Edith, theologian/philosopher Francis Schaeffer would often say, "There is a lot of leftover beauty in nature." Or as Sam said to Frodo at a point of despair in the movie adaptation of *The Two Towers*, (book two of J. R. R. Tolkien's Lord of the Rings trilogy), "There's some good in this world, and it's worth fighting for."

For our belief system to hold together, we must explain evil, but, frankly, that's not very hard. Evil wasn't part of the original plan. The answer lies in the fall. The fall of man and woman introduced every evil and bad thing that exists in creation. You'll find that event recorded in Genesis 3, where Adam and Eve were tempted and sinned. We've been sinning ever since.

Now back to question #1: Is creation good, evil, or neutral? What's *your* answer?

To See God in Creation

Now to the second question in our pop quiz: Does nature *hint of, reveal, conceal,* or *tarnish* God? Theologians describe two ways God reveals Himself to men and women. They call the Bible God's *special revelation*, and they call creation (or nature) God's *general revelation*. This is the idea that nature "reveals" a "general" knowledge about the nature and characteristics of God to everyone. As John Calvin said, "The painter reveals something of himself in his painting."

When we watch a bloodred sunset disappear over the horizon, lilies sway in a field, or baby ducks paddle for all their worth to keep up with mama duck, we also get a glimpse of God. To comprehend the visible creation is to comprehend the invisible God. We see God everywhere.

The next few paragraphs on God's works in creation deal with cultural and historical perspectives and largely reflect Schaeffer's thinking in his book *Escape from Reason*. (If you're not interested in history, you can skip to the next section.) Early in Christian history, Schaeffer notes, scholars didn't dwell much on the value of creation. You can see this reflected in a visit to a fine art museum. Before the thirteenth century, art featured high and holy subjects, but they were portrayed symbolically rather than realistically.

Then, in the thirteenth century, Thomas Aquinas arrived on the scene. Some consider Aquinas the most prominent theologian and philosopher of the Middle Ages. Aquinas lived in a time when non-Christian philosophers like Aristotle first captured the attention of cultural thinkers. They admired Aristotle's ability to explain the natural world simply through his observations, and the resulting emphasis on man's reason seemed to endanger long-held Christian beliefs.

Aquinas tried to harmonize *reason* and *revelation,* creating some unity between grace and nature (or between divine and earthly things). Because of Aquinas, people began to explore creation simply because they enjoyed it. And so, for instance, in the fourteenth century, history records that a man named Petrarch climbed a mountain just for the sake of climbing it—he had no other goal!

Then in 1410, someone drew a small landscape, the way we would see landscapes pictured today. It was only 3 x 5 inches, but it's extremely important, because it's our first example of a natural landscape painting.[2] This probably would not have happened if it hadn't been for the efforts of Aquinas to draw a connection between the temporal and the eternal.

Recall that the natural world reveals God's nature (called general revelation). For example, the first half of Psalm 19 describes how God speaks through His works (*general revelation*), and the second half about how God speaks through His Word (*specific revelation*). So Psalm 19 begins like this: "The heavens declare the glory of God; the skies proclaim the work of his hands. Day after day, they pour forth speech; night after night they display knowledge. There is no speech or language where their voice is not heard."

God doesn't merely speak through His creation—His voice erupts in peels of thunder, or whispers from the ripple of a rock that splashed into a still pond in the middle of a quiet wood. Everyone has seen God in creation. In fact, "since the creation of the world God's invisible qualities—his eternal power and divine nature—have been clearly seen, being understood from what has been made, so that men are without excuse" (Romans 1:20).

We can experience creation through our senses—we can see it, smell it, hear it, touch it, taste it. Nature will not necessarily lead us to salvation, but it will reveal God's grandeur and give us tangible evidence of His invisible qualities. As a spiritual habit, I know of no better way to experience awe than to observe God as the Creator of the heavens and earth. Through general revelation, the window is open.

So back to question #2: Does nature hint of God, reveal God, conceal God, or tarnish God? The contemplation of the visible *reveals* the deity of the invisible. The spiritual habit of observing nature leads to a deeper understanding of God.

Suggestions for Pursuing God in Creation

What's the best way to observe God in creation? Is it to gaze upon the beauty of creation? Should we look with amazement at man himself, created in God's image? Or can we stand in awe of the accomplishments of men and women? After all, people have built skyscrapers, airplanes, spaceships, televisions, telephones, and computers. They've explored new lands, naming and listing a host of animals and plants. They've found miracle medical cures. The list could go on and on. So which more clearly reveals God—raw nature, man, or man's work?

Okay, this is a trick question, because the answer is . . . we can see God in all three places. This is a powerful truth, because it frees us from the tendency to segment our lives into "Christian" and "secular" categories. We don't have to live in a world where Bible study is "Christian," therefore "good," and work is "secular," therefore "bad." Everything God made is good. First, God reveals Himself in creation. Second, He reveals Himself through His reflection in mankind. And third, He reveals Himself through our accomplishments as well.

Pursue God's Creation through Nature

You may put this book down and walk outside to enjoy the beauty of your yard. You might go to the mountains or to the beach for a weekend break. Perhaps you live in a city, but you can still do what I love to do— look up at the nighttime sky and admire the stars.

I love sitting in my backyard before dawn and gazing up into the sky. In that quiet moment, when a tangible hush rests on my neighborhood, before the kitchen lights announce the day's beginning and before the engines rev and car doors begin slamming on my street, I think about Psalm 8: "When I consider your heavens, the work of your fingers, the moon and the stars, which you have set in place, what is man that you are mindful of him, the son of man that you care for him?" (verses 3–4).

You can pick up a book about any topic, and you will find that it communicates something about its author. Similarly, creation offers its own message of beauty and grandeur, and it also communicates something about its Creator. It gives perspective. Nature reveals God's invisible qualities, His eternal and infinite power, His divine nature. When I sit in my backyard and stare at the stars and the planets and the moon, I am humbled by God's greatness. Yet I also am encouraged by His willingness to stoop into my world and pursue me.

Pursue God's Creation through Man's Work

Raw nature has the power to turn our thoughts to God, but so do manmade things. Consider, for instance, the intricacy of a fine watch, the grandeur of a skyscraper, the glorious sound of a symphony, the hum of a finely tuned engine, the delicious smell of steaks on the grill. I love driving through beautiful neighborhoods and admiring the homes, manicured lawns, and flower gardens. I love the smell of freshly mown grass and the restful simplicity of a well-designed golf course. This list is almost endless: parks, sculpture, art, music, cathedrals, computers, the muscular curves of a Porsche.

God uses our works to echo His own character throughout the world. Who doesn't marvel at the power of a laptop computer or PDA? How did that happen? It is a reflection of God's own creative character, which He has put in human beings.

Pursue God's Creation by Observing His Human Creation

Beyond raw nature and man's work lies the wonder of how God has handcrafted people. Who doesn't admire a beautiful woman or a handsome man? We love to recognize and reward human achievement. In the creative arts, we have Emmys, Oscars, Tonys, and People's Choice awards. We can't wait to celebrate the athletic exploits of people like Lance Armstrong and Jeff Gordon and to present Espys to outstanding athletes.

One man may not appear very talented when compared to another man, but both will appear quite talented when compared to a rabbit or a dancing bear. The least human being is infinitely more interesting than the highest beast in creation. Every human being—whether beautiful or talented or athletic—is part of the creation and, when pondered, can turn our thoughts to the greatness of God.

Whether you're focusing on natural beauty, man-made beauty, or mankind's beauty, let the result be the same—let it propel your mind to meditate on the greatness and goodness of the holy God. In *The Idea of the Holy* Rudolph Otto summed it up well, as he described what he called the *mysterium tremendum*, the presence of the transcendent One:

> The feeling of it at times may come sweeping like a gentle tide, pervading the mind with a tranquil mood of deepest worship. It may pass over into a more set and lasting attitude of the soul, continuing, as it were, thrillingly vibrant and resonant, until at last it dies away and the soul resumes its 'profane,' non-religious mood of everyday experience. It may burst in sudden eruption up from the depths of the soul with spasms and convulsions, or lead to the strangest excitements, to intoxicated frenzy, to transport, and to ecstasy. . . . It may become the hushed, trembling, and speechless humility of the creature in the presence of—whom or what? In the presence of that which is a *mystery* inexpressible and above all creatures.[3]

That's what we're looking for in contemplating nature—the experience of God's holiness. When you find it in creation, how should you respond? Do not fall in the trap described in Romans 1:21: "For although they knew God, they neither glorified him as God nor gave thanks to him." Instead, glorify God; give thanks to God. That's why we want to cultivate these habits—so we can come to a place where we voluntarily glorify God and give Him thanks.

A Suggested Spiritual Exercise

- Sit quietly in a quiet room at a quiet time of the day.

- Become aware of everything in the room—the noises, the silence, the creaks, the wind outside or lack of it, a draft, the humidity, the temperature, your body, the furniture, the light, each chair, fabric, texture, color, and how these things make you feel.

- Consider what else is in the room that you cannot see—radio waves, TV waves, microwaves, cellular phone conversations, Internet transmissions.

- Next, become aware of the Spirit of God in the room—in the same sense that He was always there even when you were not focused on Him.

- Pray, "Jesus, I know that You are right here with me. May I sense Your presence."

Other Suggested Spiritual Exercises

- Sit quietly in the predawn hour gazing into the sky.

- Watch a vermillion sky yield to a new day, or to darkness.

- Go sit still beside a stream. Listen to the rippling water and the sounds beyond it . . . the birds, the rustling leaves.

- Watch an anthill.

- Stare back at a heron.

- Marvel at the mating ritual of two birds.

- Look at a mountain and think how long it would take one person to cart it away, or make one, or climb it.

- Consider a mother duck and her little chicks.

Heavenly Father, we do worship You, we do glorify You, we do give You thanks, and we do see You in creation. We see You everywhere around us. We see You in people. We see You in things made well by man. We see You in nature, and it is good, and we acknowledge that You have revealed Yourself to us. Lord, give us the habit or the discipline to come often to this place, to this attitude, to this mind-set so that we might be with You, that we might have communion with You and that our relationship with You might deepen. We ask this in the name and the power of the invisible God made visible in creation. Amen.

A Review of the Big Ideas

The contemplation of the visible creation reveals the deity of the invisible God.

When we watch a bloodred sunset disappear over the horizon, lilies sway in a field, or baby ducks paddle for all their worth to keep up with mama duck, we also get a glimpse of God.

The spiritual habit of observing nature leads to a deeper understanding of God.

You can pick up a book about any topic, and you will find that it communicates something about its author. Similarly, creation offers its own message of beauty and grandeur, and it also communicates something about its Creator.

Whether you're focusing on natural beauty, man-made beauty, or mankind's beauty, let the result be the same—let it propel your mind to meditate on the greatness and goodness of the holy God.

Discussion Questions

1. Look up the creation story in Genesis 1—especially look at verses 10, 12, 18, 21, 25, 31. What do you see in each of those verses? What does that tell you about God's creation?

2. Look up Psalm 139—especially look at verses 13–16. What does that tell you about yourself?

3. Describe your last experience of interaction with God's creation.

4. What did that experience teach you about God?

5. We've described ways to experience God through nature, through people, and through accomplishments. Which of those ways most clearly gives you a sense of God's majesty? Which most clearly gives you a sense of His presence?

Additional Resources

Escape from Reason, by Francis Schaeffer (especially for more information about nature, grace, and Aquinas)

The Problem of Pain, by C. S. Lewis

The Idea of the Holy, by Rudolph Otto

www.kenduncan.com (a commercial Web site for Christian photographer Ken Duncan, whose pictures will inspire you and turn your thoughts to God)

PART TWO

DISCIPLINE RELATED TO THE WORD OF GOD

A MAN AND THE BIBLE

PREVIEW

In this chapter we will learn the importance of reading the Bible and how to develop the habit of regular study and devotion time. We'll:

- **Understand that the Bible actually is God's Word.**
- **Learn the Bible's purpose.**
- **Discover practical ideas about how to read your Bible—when, where, and how often.**

When professional golfer Vijay Singh won the Masters, he was playing with a note pinned to his golf bag. It was from his ten-year-old son Qass, and it said, "Daddy, trust your swing." Because he had practiced and trained, Vijay could take his son's advice. His swing brought him victory.

When you're at the driving range or on the golf course, you can usually tell if a man has taken golfing lessons just by watching how he swings. For the most part, no training (or bad training) yields an unproductive swing. Lessons from a golf pro—someone who has invested a great deal of time and effort in learning to play effectively—can yield a productive swing, if the student follows instruction and practices.

Now imagine this: What if Vijay Singh called you and said, "I'm in your area tomorrow. How would you like me to give you a free golf lesson?" Do you think that would motivate you to show up for a lesson? To listen to his instruction? And to practice what he teaches?

In the spiritual realm, we all have a similar privilege. As Christians, we are called to live as Jesus did. You may be thinking, *I don't even know what that means!* Clearly, Jesus is the best instructor, and He is willing to teach. He will be "in your area tomorrow." Or you can meet with Him tonight. He is ready to give you a lesson. That lesson will begin with reading and studying your Bible.

What Is Bible Study?

In 2 Timothy 2:15, Paul wrote to his spiritual son, saying, "Do your best to present yourself to God as one approved, a workman who does not need to be ashamed and who correctly handles the word of truth." According to the Greek dictionary in *Strong's Exhaustive Concordance*, the word that we've translated *correctly handles* literally means "to make a straight cut or to dissect." That implies more than just a cursory knowledge of a subject. It indicates someone investing substantial time, thought, and effort into the subject.

Bible *reading* is always a good habit. But Bible *study* implies something very different. It indicates we aren't flying through the Bible so we can check off a list that says we've read so many chapters in so many days. Rather, we read and "dissect" the teaching—mull it over—so we can apply it to our lives.

Can We Trust the Bible?

Of course, anyone who takes the Bible seriously must begin by believing it is God's communication. Where does that confidence begin?

First of all, the Bible does claim to be the Word of God. More than 3,800 times, authors introduce a passage with a phrase like, "Thus says the Lord," or "The Lord spoke." Some prophets even claimed they were under direct orders from God, compelled to give His message. Jesus quoted passages from the Old Testament, verifying their origin as coming from God.[1]

Jesus also quoted the Old Testament as having authority in His day. For example, when He chased the money changers from the temple, He quoted Isaiah 56:7 and Jeremiah 7:11. "'It is written,' he said to them, 'My house will be a house of prayer'; but you have made it 'a den of robbers'" (Luke 19:46). Jesus also cited the authority of Moses when He proclaimed the validity of His own ministry: "If you believed Moses, you would believe me, for he wrote about me" (John 5:46).

In just these two verses—Luke 19:46 and John 5:46—Jesus authenticated the writings of Moses (Genesis, Exodus, Leviticus, Numbers, and Deuteronomy) and also the prophets Jeremiah and Isaiah—seven of the Bible's sixty-six books.

Consider what information the following verses give us about the authenticity and power of Scripture:

All Scripture is God-breathed and is useful for teaching, rebuking, correcting and training in righteousness, so that the man of God may be thoroughly equipped for every good work. (2 Timothy 3:16–17)

Every word of God is flawless; he is a shield to those who take refuge in him. Do not add to his words, or he will rebuke you and prove you a liar. (Proverbs 30:5–6)

The internal witness is clear: The Bible claims that Scripture comes from God and is without error.

Now, it's certainly true that an internal claim is not necessarily accurate. If I claim to be the king of England, that doesn't make me the king. Yet it is not insignificant that the Bible does claim to be "the Word of God." We do have quite a bit of empirical evidence to support the internal claim. For example, consider that the Bible is made up of sixty-six different books from over forty different human authors, written over fifteen centuries. Yet it flows with such continuity that it looks like a single piece of cloth. That's difficult to explain outside of God's guiding in the process.

And we have 5,659 partial or complete Greek New Testament manuscripts in existence. Compare that with only five, six, or seven copies of Plato and nine or ten copies of Julius Caesar.[2] Yet most scholars have no difficulty accepting the veracity of Plato and Caesar on just those few manuscripts. The continuity of content and manuscript evidence alone are strong indicators that Scripture came from God.

Then there's the whole process (by the early church) that established what texts were included in our Bible. A *canon* is a theological word for an authoritative list of books accepted as Scripture. The Old Testament canon was pretty well set by 300 BC. The New Testament canon was already taking shape by the end of the first century. Thirteen of Paul's letters were in circulation, and churches began collecting copies and archiving them. Also, many gospels were circulating by the end of the first century and the beginning of the second century. Early church leaders were already figuring out which of these writings were authentic and which were not. So by the end of the second century, the four gospels were accepted as the written Word of God.

There were naysayers, however. We know that an influential man named Marcion challenged "the included list." He rejected the Old Testament entirely. He accepted as Scripture only edited versions of Luke's gospel and ten of Paul's letters. Before the middle of the second century, Marcion appeared at a hearing before the clergy of Rome's congregations. That hearing resulted in a rejection of his views. Even though the process of establishing the canon had already begun, Marcion's suggestions forced a formal response, thus accelerating the finalization of the canon of the Bible.

By the end of the fourth century, there were two important church meetings—the Council of Laodicea in 363, and the Council at Carthage in 397. Both gave canonical lists that mirrored what was already accepted in the church. We also know that Athanasius, the bishop in Alexandria, Egypt, had a tradition of writing an Easter letter every year. In his Easter epistle of 367, he acknowledged the twenty-seven books that we have in our New Testament. He testified to their authenticity and authority.

So the books included in our Old and New Testaments have been recognized by internal and external testimony. Christian leaders through the ages have agreed that what is included in our Bible did originate with God, and it is a trustworthy document. Tens of thousands of scholars have spent millions of hours and dollars studying the Bible's credibility. They agree—it really is God's Word.

Why Is Bible Study Important?

In studying the Bible, we should remember that Scripture has a purpose. The gospel of John was written by one of Jesus' disciples—a close friend who knew our Lord personally. Toward the end of his book the apostle John explained why his account was selective: "Jesus did many other miraculous signs in the presence of his disciples, which are not recorded in this book. But these are written that you may believe that Jesus is the Christ, the Son of God, and that by believing you may have life in his name" (John 20:30–31).

A 1994 study revealed that 73 percent of Americans believe all the miracles in the Bible took place exactly as they are stated. Yet by looking at our culture, most of us would agree that belief hasn't changed how people think or behave. John said he recorded those miracles for a purpose. He intended for his readers to understand and accept that Jesus is the Messiah —the Savior—and to know that He is God's Son.

Why is that important? Because belief gives birth to life. Theologians say that Scriptures are given for our *justification* and *sanctification*. That basically means the Bible exists to bring us to faith (justification, or salvation), and to help us become more and more like Christ as we grow up in our faith (sanctification, or holiness). We see that sanctification process modeled in Psalm 1. This passage carries a promise for the man who plugs into God's Word. Psalm 1:1–3 tells us,

Blessed is the man who does not walk in the counsel of the wicked or
stand in the way of sinners or sit in the seat of mockers. But his delight
is in the law of the LORD, and on his law he meditates day and night. He
is like a tree planted by streams of water, which yields its fruit in season
and whose leaf does not wither. Whatever he does prospers.

Now, let's go back and dissect that passage. It begins with a progression of activity—walking, standing, and sitting. That seems to indicate that a man who does not pursue God's Word is in danger of progressively getting more involved and comfortable with sinful ways. But the man who delights in—that is, values, desires, willingly pursues—God's Word is on a very different path. He walks toward fruitfulness and prosperity. Bible study is important, because it helps us discern and follow God's plan.

Living Out a Commitment to Scripture

I'm extremely proud of my son, because he has decided he's going to be a man of God's Word, like the man described in Psalm 1. He has made God's Word his standard. My son married a while ago. One of his grooms-men is the son of my wife's good friend. So she was asking her son, the groomsman, "What are you going to do for the bachelor party? Are you going to get a stripper and a keg of beer?"

He said, "Mom, we're not going to do any of those things. John Mor-ley is cut out of a different kind of cloth than that. We'll probably watch the Beverly Hillbillies movie or something."

When my son was growing up, I paid him (and my daughter!) to read the Bible every day. It was a good investment, because now he has become a man of God's Word. When he went off to college, he kept reading his Bible. Not only that, but he found a church and joined a campus ministry. He taught four or five high schoolers every Thursday morning in a Bible study in a local restaurant. (My daughter took a similar path).

My son is like that tree planted by a stream of water whose leaf does not wither, and everything he is doing right now is positive. Does that mean he's not going to have hard times and suffering? Of course not! But on bal-ance, here is a young man who is experiencing the promise of applying the spiritual discipline of God's Word. He demonstrates that it's possible. God's Word is available to all of us. The question is, are we available to God's Word?

Suggestions for Pursuing the Discipline of Bible Study

We've established that the Bible is God's Word. If you believe that, doesn't it make sense that you'd want to read it? Francis Bacon said, "Read-ing maketh a full man; conference maketh a ready man; and writing maketh an exact man." My first suggestion to you is *read* the Bible. Charles Spurgeon lamented that he could find ten men who were willing to die for the Bible for every one who was actually willing to read it. Don't just leave it on your shelf or even carry it around in your briefcase. Read it.

Here are a few practical suggestions to help you in regular, meaningful Bible study.

1. Get a small Bible.

Get a small Bible that you can keep in your pocket or Bible software for your PDA. Early in my career, when I was out selling, I was often going to see people who didn't want to see me. I knew that sometimes I'd have a long wait in a reception room, frequently as much as thirty minutes. Since I persisted in getting the appointment, I always suspected they wanted me to wait to make sure I appreciated it! So I carried a little Bible in my pocket, and during those waiting times, I read it over and over again. Today I have two versions of the Bible in my PDA. I use Laridian (www.laridian.com).

You may think, *I don't have time to read my Bible*. But you can. Get yourself a small Bible, and read while you're waiting for flights, for appointments, for carpooling buddies, or for . . . You get the point. If you really think it through, you can find some time.

2. Get the One Year Bible.

The One Year Bible (published by Tyndale) follows the calendar and gives you a reading for each day. By the end of the year, you've read the whole thing. I've done this for more than twenty years. It gives me a strategy to read the entire Bible—cover to cover—at least one time every year. You can purchase a hard copy or find a one-year reading plan at www.oneyearbibleonline.com.

3. Set a regular time for daily Bible reading and study.

Set that appointment for Bible reading and study at a time each day when you are not easily distracted. What distracts you? For me, if I start doing "anything" else first, I find it difficult to settle down and still my mind for reading, study, communion, and reflection. I am not the only one who knows this; so does my adversary, the Devil. Prayer is about the only way that I can refocus my attention. I like the Lord's Prayer. But it's better not to have to refocus in the first place by being consistent!

Personally, I like getting up early to read and study. Three days a week I spend one hour on an exercise bicycle, so I read my Bible while I'm at it. It's multitasking, and it feels great. The other days I sit quietly and read at my desk.

Take the five-minute challenge! If you don't have a consistent quiet time, set aside five minutes daily to read a chapter in the Bible and say a prayer. Start by reading a chapter in the New Testament. The New Testament has 260 chapters. So if you take five minutes a day to read a chapter, five days a week, you can read through the New Testament in one year. Wouldn't that be an affirming accomplishment? Underline passages that capture your attention. Write those texts on a 3 x 5 card, carry them with you, and memorize them for strength, courage, and faith.

4. Meet with other Christians to study the Bible.

Remember what Bacon said? He said that reading maketh a full man and conference maketh a ready man. He was saying that reading will fill you up, but to be ready to do something about it is the result of meeting with others.

My brother, Pete, became a follower of Jesus Christ several years ago. For the first half-dozen years, I kept wondering about his commitment. I said to myself, "You know, I hear the professions, but I don't see much to recommend the message."

Then he got involved in a small-group men's Bible study in his church, and he has been transformed. Literally, he is a different person, because he has opened himself to God's Word, and he has allowed it to modify the way he thinks and behaves.

Get into a Bible study with other men or couples. It will help you move beyond reading and reflection to application. A Christian without a Bible study group is like a violinist without an orchestra, a football player without a team, or a businessman without a company.

A Changed Life

I have never known any man whose life changed in any significant way apart from the regular study of God's Word. The Bible, once accepted, demands a response. The Old Testament prophet Isaiah wrote this on God's behalf: "My word that goes out from my mouth . . . will not return to me empty, but will accomplish what I desire and achieve the purpose for which I sent it" (Isaiah 55:11).

That's what's happening in my brother, Pete's, life. That's what can happen in your life. Read your Bible. Bible study is training. It's the spiritual equivalent of sports training. A golfer who doesn't receive training on how to swing a club will nonetheless develop a habit of swinging and certain beliefs about why to do so in a particular way, whether well founded or not. Likewise, a convert who doesn't receive training on how to be a disciple will nonetheless take on certain spiritual habits and beliefs, whether well founded or not. And as we all know, it is much more difficult to unlearn a bad habit than to learn it right the first time. Sometimes what we end up doing is teaching old dogs new tricks.

If you want to play well at this idea of Christianity, and you want to have a good "swing," then you have to show up for your lesson, listen to the instruction, and practice. The Bible is the starting point for all spiritual discipline, for everything that glorifies God, for all communion with Jesus Christ, and for all growth and sanctification. If I could make only one recommendation to a man for how to improve his life, I would say, first, read the Bible for yourself every day. My second recommendation? Get in a small group to study it together.

I like to write books. It's very exciting when someone comes to me and says, "I read your book, and I really liked it." However, I've noticed that people comment about my books in different ways. One man said, "I have that book." Several men have said, "I've been meaning to read that book."

It doesn't have the same impact as when a man says, "Oh, yes. I've read that book! I like that book!"

Someday soon you're going to meet the Bible's author. What if He says to you, "How did you like My book?" Do you want to say, "I have that book" or "I've been meaning to read that!" Or do you want to say, "Oh, yes. I've read that book! That book changed my life!"

Heavenly Father, Your Word is powerful. Your Word has wonder-ful purpose. Your Word has wonderful promises. We can have great confidence that when You speak, we can trust what You say. I pray that each of us would have the highest possible regard for Your Word. Use Your Word to mold us and prepare us for the challenges we face. In Christ's name we pray. Amen.

A Review of the Big Ideas

༄ It is not insignificant that the Bible claims to be "the Word of God."

༄ Tens of thousands of scholars have spent millions of hours and dollars studying the Bible's credibility. They agree—it really is God's Word.

༄ Get a small Bible that you can keep in your pocket or Bible software for your handheld device.

༄ Get the One Year Bible.

༄ Meet with other Christians to study the Bible.

༄ Set a regular appointment with yourself to read and study your Bible each day at a time when you are not easily distracted.

༄ I have never known any man whose life changed in any significant way apart from his regular study of God's Word.

Discussion Questions

1. Name an athlete you really admire. Why do you admire him? How do you think he has prepared to be successful in his sport? How does that compare to preparing for success in the Christian life? (See 1 Corinthians 9:24–25; 1 Timothy 4:7; 2 Timothy 4:7–8, Hebrews 12:1–2.)

2. What is the role of Bible reading in that training process? (See Joshua 1:6–9; Psalm 119:9–16, 24; 2 Timothy 3:15–17.)

3. Circle the number that represents how many days per week you read at least some portion of Scripture.

0   1   2   3   4   5   6   7

4. Do you think the amount of time you spend reading the Bible is helping or hurting your preparation for living the Christian life?

5. If you believe you need to do better in the area of Bible reading, list at least one step you can take to improve. (Remember—there are some practical suggestions in "Suggestions for Pursuing the Discipline of Bible Study.)

Additional Resources

Visit the Resource Center and Bookstore at www.maninthemirror.org and find over five hundred free articles, Bibles, printed Bible study resources, and the free weekly Webcasts of the Man in the Mirror Bible Study that I teach each week. For the Bible study Webcasts you can download or stream the messages in video or audio, and you can download the same small-group discussion questions we use here in Orlando. (Those questions are similar to the questions at the end of each chapter in this book.) You can also podcast the weekly messages.

PART THREE

DISCIPLINES RELATED TO THE "WHISPER" OF GOD

A MAN AND PRAYER

PREVIEW

In this chapter, we will explore how prayer can be a two-way conversation rather than a one-way monologue. We'll:

- Discover what it means to pray "a little" or to pray "a lot."
- Discuss why prayer is an important habit for a man trying to become more like Christ.
- Determine multiple ways to incorporate this discipline into your daily life.

Over the Christmas holidays one year, our family and my wife's extended family—twelve of us—went to New York. The highlight of our visit was a tour of the 9-11 site. But we also went to see a play, *The Music Man*.

Through a web of relationships, we ended up backstage. I discovered something—there's a huge difference between sitting in an audience watching people act out a story, and actually conversing with the lead actor or actress.

The woman who played the lead had also played Christine in *Phantom of the Opera*. I had admired this woman since the first time I heard her voice (I have her on my iPod), and now I was going to meet her. To be honest, it was a little intimidating. Yet she was so warm and friendly that we all felt instantly at ease. She wanted to know all about us!

Let's apply that principle to our relationship with God. In the first chapter we discussed the habit of looking at God's creation to see His character. We noted that we can relate more closely to Him as we admire His handiwork. That's like watching the play from the audience. But He also extends the spiritual equivalent of a backstage invitation. He wants to chat—to have an actual conversation. That's amazing. And having a conversation regularly is a beneficial habit to cultivate.

What Is Prayer?

Jonathan Edwards wrote, "The substance of religion is conscious communion with God." In his book *Celebration of Discipline*, Richard Foster makes the statement, "Of all the spiritual disciplines, prayer is most central because it ushers in perpetual communion with the Father." So the substance of religion for Edwards is conscious communion with God. And, according to Foster, prayer is the best avenue for ongoing communion with our Father.

Most men who pick up this book are already investing themselves to some degree in prayer. Most of us already know the merits of praying. But that general observation creates a puzzle. Some men act on that knowledge, and they pray a lot. Others don't act on that knowledge, and they pray only a little. Why is that true?

To answer that, let's begin by defining terms. I see prayer as the conversation that turns salvation into a close personal relationship with God. So when I say "a little" and "a lot," I'm not necessarily referring to a quantity of time spent in praying. Some people talk a lot without actually saying much. Others say a lot in just a few words. Praying "a little" or "a lot" has more to do with the level of intimacy or communion attained through prayer.

Some men might object to the word *intimacy*. But I think a secure man can admit that what he craves is a close relationship with God. Prayer is an important part of how we make that happen. Real prayer is a two-way conversation. Certainly we talk to God, but we also listen. Think about how boring it is when you go to lunch with someone who does nothing but talk. The result isn't a conversation—it's a monologue. When I refer to a man who prays a lot, I'm talking about a guy whose prayer is a conversation. I'm not talking about someone who prattles on incessantly at God.

Why Should We Pray?

Most people pray because they want to receive. They ask God to meet needs and/or desires. Frankly, God invites us to do that, so let's not demean that as a motivation. Let's just say it's not the only motivation. As we've already noted, prayer is a primary venue for developing intimacy with God. That's a precious gift. So why do so many men resist praying?

I can only answer that for myself. When I refuse to pray, I sometimes find I've been subconsciously trying to "get back at God" for not doing what I wanted Him to do. In that emotional moment, it seems less than Christian to feel this way, so I suppress it. The problem is, it still comes out in my behavior—I avoid communication. This is, of course, a form of passive-aggressive resistance.

It's not an unusual response. In fact, we see it occasionally in biblical characters. For instance, look at the prophet Jonah. God gave him a job he didn't like, so he sulked. He quit communicating and tried to run away. He boarded a ship to go in exactly the opposite direction from the place God had directed him. He ended up in a storm, was thrown overboard, and was swallowed by a fish before he finally repented and resumed praying.

Hopefully you and I will not require that kind of drastic measure when we need to repent and seek to restore our relationship with God. The risk of not praying is not only that you may not get what you want, but that you get what you don't want. Jonah is a clear example of that.

If you sense you are "shutting down" in this area, please be honest. Go ahead and tell God, "You know, I'm really angry with You about this right now." (Or perhaps you are hurt, disappointed, frustrated, scared, confused, doubtful . . . You fill in the emotion.) Honest communication in prayer is much more healthy than the alternative.

Living Out a Commitment to Prayer

From the day of my salvation I wanted to relate with God at an intimate level. I knew that would be accomplished through developing a habit of prayer, so I invested quite a bit of time in studying men who pray "a lot." I found those men in Scripture, in literature, and in contemporary life. From their examples, I found three characteristics: (1) These men spent time in the "school of prayer." (2) They've come to see prayer as the most powerful and efficient use of their time. (3) They've made prayer their first disposition. Let's look at those three characteristics more closely.

1. Time in the School of Prayer

In Luke 11:1 the disciples said to Jesus, "Lord, teach us to pray." There is a language of prayer. You can pray the way Jesus prayed by studying His prayers. Emulate other men who pray with authenticity. And read some of the great saints on prayer—Andrew Murray's classic 1885 book, *With Christ in the School of Prayer*, is one of many wonderful books that you can check out. Beyond the words of Jesus, also watch for the attitude of His heart.

I live near a lake where I've been rowing a scull for several years. This vessel is twenty-five feet long and, fully rigged, weighs only forty-two pounds. In the first year I took a couple of lessons.

One day a neighbor told me, "You know, you really look so peaceful out there when you're rowing. You look so calm." Let me tell you what's really going on out there. This twenty-five-foot toothpick is very tippy. It has no stability, always wanting to plunk me into the water. I replied, "I don't feel so peaceful. I'm hanging on for dear life!" The reason I'm hanging on is that, basically, I haven't learned anything new since my first year.

Practice does not necessarily mean progress. Until I learn something new about the art of rowing, I probably won't get any better. The last few years have proven that, because I've been out there flopping around like a fish, barely keeping it upright.

The same can be said of prayer. Someone can pray—they can even say a lot when they pray—but that doesn't mean they're really good at it. To get better, we need to sit with Jesus in the school of prayer. That means we study His Word to discover the "how to" of conversation with Him.

Here's an example. Early one day on their way to the temple, Jesus and His disciples passed a fig tree that had no fruit on it. Jesus cursed the tree, and by the next morning, that tree had withered. Peter noticed it and commented. Here's Jesus' response:

> "Have faith in God," Jesus answered. "I tell you the truth, if anyone says to this mountain, 'Go, throw yourself into the sea,' . . . it will be done for him. Therefore I tell you, whatever you ask for in prayer, believe that you have received it, and it will be yours. And when you stand praying, if you hold anything against anyone, forgive him, so that your Father in heaven may forgive you your sins." (Mark 11:22–26)

That passage provides great motivation for prayer. Yet we've all been through situations where we asked and did not receive. Why?

Let's sit in the school of prayer and put that side by side with James 4:3, which says, "When you ask, you do not receive, because you ask with wrong motives, that you may spend what you get on your pleasures."

As men, we experience a lifelong tug-of-war between James 4:3 and Mark 11. The juxtaposition of the two passages reveals the difference between prayer that wells up from the flesh, and prayer that flows from relationship with God's Spirit. As we ponder these concepts, we will begin to conquer some of our misconceptions about how prayer works. That's an example of what it means to sit with Jesus in the school of prayer.

2. Prayer as a Powerful Use of Time

Learn to see prayer as the most powerful and efficient use of your time. In the physical world, ideas are more powerful than labor, because ideas propel motion. Once the energy is released, it can't be contained. Prayer also is more powerful than labor, because it also releases forces that will not be contained.

Martin Luther is famous for commenting, "I have so much to do today that I'm going to need to spend three hours in prayer in order to be able to get it all done." So why is it so hard to accept that prayer is the most powerful investment of time? The answer is simple—it doesn't look as if it works. We don't always get what we pray for.

When we work, we earn a specific reward. The equation goes like this:

effort + work = reaching my goal

On the surface, human effort seems more profitable than prayer. For a lot of us, prayer seems spiritual and mystical. We don't understand it. We don't want to risk not getting what we pray for. So we pray a little and work a lot.

Summers are financial agony for anyone in ministry, because contributions naturally fall off in that season. That's as true for us at Man in the Mirror as it is for the next ministry.

One summer in particular, finances were really tight. I started praying, and I ran across two key Scripture passages. Philippians 4:19 says, "And my God will meet all your needs according to his glorious riches in Christ Jesus." Then Matthew 6:31–32 records Jesus saying, "So do not worry, saying, 'What shall we eat?' or 'What shall we drink?' or 'What shall we wear?' For the pagans run after all these things, and your Father knows that you need them." Then it says we are to seek God's kingdom first and quit worrying.

In the practical world, that's hard to do. The ministry I serve has thirty staff members. They have mortgage payments, rent payments, and car payments. They have to buy groceries and pay for childcare, gasoline, and doctor bills. Those staff members depend on their salaries. One week in that particular summer, we had absolutely nothing to cover payroll. We had some meetings, and I went home, and I wrote in my journal, "God, I feel like You have failed me. I don't believe that You failed me, but that is how I feel."

You might have already guessed that God did meet that need, and

He's met every other need. But we all have moments when life just doesn't work the way we expect it to. In those moments we must be confident that prayer is the most powerful and efficient use of time.

Blaise Pascal said, "God instituted prayer in order to allow his creatures the dignity of causality." C. S. Lewis said,

> The two methods by which we are allowed to produce events may be called work and prayer. . . . The kind of causality we exercise by work is, so to speak, divinely guaranteed, and therefore ruthless. By it we are free to do ourselves as much harm as we please. But the kind which we exercise by prayer it not like that; God has left Himself a discretionary power. Had He not done so, prayer would be an activity too dangerous for man. . . . That is why God has retained a discretionary power of granting or refusing it; except on that condition prayer would destroy us.[1]

In other words, prayer is so much more powerful than labor that God has put some limitations on it. If He hadn't done that, we'd all destroy ourselves. Lewis then gives this wonderful illustration:

> It is not unreasonable for a headmaster to say, "Such and such things you may do according to the fixed rules of this school. But such and such other things are too dangerous to be left to general rules. If you want to do them you must come and make a request and talk over the whole matter with me in my study. And then— we'll see."[2]

Do you trust God enough to understand that He already knows everything you need before you pray for it? That's what the Scriptures say. He's going to give you everything you need out of His glorious riches. And He will answer every prayer that you go into His study to explore with Him—sometimes yes, sometimes no.

So recognize prayer as the most powerful and efficient use of your time. A young businessman told me, "You know, I really don't have a lot of time for prayer and Bible reading. I have young kids, I'm building my career, and I'm very active in my church." I'd suggest he should realign his priorities.

When I was in that same mind-set, I took a suggestion from management guru Peter Drucker. I sat down with a piece of paper and charted how I actually spent my time. Drucker says everyone has expectations about what their chart will say, and without exception, everyone is surprised by what they actually find. I discovered that I spent one to two hours every night watching television. I started going to bed early instead of watching TV, and getting up two hours earlier in the morning. People sometimes think I'm crazy to get up at 4 a.m., but that's okay. I'm in conversation with God.

If you really want to do this, you'll find a way. If you want a close relationship with Jesus, you can have it, but you must cultivate that relationship through conversation.

3. Prayer—The First Priority

Make prayer your first disposition. In 1 Samuel 14, Scripture records a battle between the Israelites and the Philistines. Saul was Israel's king at the time, and his army was routing the enemy. In verse 36 Saul said, "Let us go down after the Philistines by night and plunder them till dawn, and let us not leave one of them alive." His men agreed, saying they'd do whatever he thought best. But the priest said, "Let's ask God first."

That summarizes the tendency that eventually led to Saul's demise. He never made prayer his first disposition. Prayer was not ingrained in him until it became a habit—an immediate response. King Saul lost that tug-of-war over and over again. As we read the Old Testament we see, of course, that David was the man who eventually replaced Saul. David's automatic tendency was to request God's wisdom and direction. The man who prays a lot will cultivate this same attitude. He will make prayer his habit. It will be his priority; he will be disposed to prayer.

Suggestions for Pursuing the Discipline of Prayer

1. Develop a quiet time that includes prayer.

A "quiet time" of Bible readings and reflection should include daily prayer, and you should change that quiet time when it gets overly routine. Over the years, lots of prayer warriors have developed systems or methods or formulas that have helped them focus on prayer. In my opinion, they all have some value, and the best method is the one you will use.

Over the last few years, I've pretty consistently used the Lord's Prayer, "Our Father which art in heaven" (Matthew 6:9ff. KJV). I pray through a phrase of it, reflect, and then pray about the things the Lord brings to mind that correspond with that list. Here are three examples to focus on:

> "Give us this day our daily bread." That leads me to pray about the areas where my family, friends, staff, and I need God's provision.

> "Forgive us our debts as we have forgiven our debtors." That leads me to pray about areas where I need to repent, but also where I need to let someone else "off the hook" for something that has hurt me or made me angry.

> "Lead us not into temptation, but deliver us from evil." That leads me to pray for protection in areas where I know I am susceptible to temptation.

Perhaps that would work for you. Or you may prefer another approach—like the acrostic ACTS:

> **A** is *adoration.* Worship God for His attributes—His holiness, power, majesty, beauty, kindness, mercy, and goodness.

> **C** is *confession.* Confess and ask God to forgive all known sin; keep "short accounts" with God.

T is *thanksgiving*. Express gratitude to God for His blessings and mercies, especially things we ordinarily take for granted, such as a good night's rest, daily provision, health, family, and so on.

S is *supplication*. Nothing is too big or too insignificant to bring to God in prayer.

Lorne Sanny, former president of the Navigators, suggested we pray backward through yesterday's events step by step, and forward through today's. Praying backward will lead to prayers of thanksgiving and confession, while praying forward will lead to prayers of supplication.

You might want to have specific lists of things. For example, I produced a list I used to pray for my children when they were growing up.[3]

You might want to keep a prayer journal. There are no rules here except that prayer is a conversation intended to turn your salvation into a close communion and intimate relationship with our Lord and Savior Jesus Christ.

2. Pray about everything.

The Bible is very clear that we are to pray about everything. Actually, a quiet time is an accommodation to overly busy people. The biblical concept is to "pray without ceasing" and meditate on God's Word "day and night" (1 Thessalonians 5:18; Psalm 1:2). The man who wears the armor of God still needs prayer, the apostle Paul wrote, and he should pray "on all occasions with all kinds of prayers and requests" (Ephesians 6:18).

3. Pray regularly with your wife (if married) or an accountability partner.

If married, try praying with your wife every day. Although marriage and prayer statistics are hotly debated, Dr. Tom Elliff, chairman of the Southern Baptist Council on the Family, notes how prayer coupled with regular church attendance and counseling benefits a marriage: "What we have discovered, however, is this: born-again Christian couples who marry . . . in the church after having received premarital counseling . . . and attend church regularly and pray daily together, that the divorce rate is approximately 1 divorce out of nearly 39,000."[4]

Whatever the statistical significance, praying with your wife symbolizes a depth of relationship with God and each other. Shaun, from Bozeman, Montana, asked his men's group, "How many of you pray with your wives?" Only one of the eight men answered, yes. For the next year they held each other accountable. As one of the men said, "It's pretty hard to be upset with your wife or to be arguing and still come before God with a clean heart. It forces us to communicate and humble ourselves before each other before we do something as intimate as praying together. It just permeates through the rest of your family, and day."

Here's an idea: Ask your wife if you can take two or three minutes each day, maybe before work, for (a) praising and thanking God, (b) intervention, and (c) intercession.

If you are single or want more prayer with another person, meet with a man to pray. A number of men I know have prayer partners. Some meet at set times; others call each other when specific needs come up. A married man should never have a woman other than his wife as a prayer partner. A single man should never have a married woman as a prayer partner.

Suggested Spiritual Exercises

- Spend some time every day pouring out your heart to God. Then intentionally quiet yourself to discern impressions from the Holy Spirit (that agree with God's Word).

- Look up the verses in Discussion Question #1 below, and ask God to give you the desire to make prayer the first disposition of your heart.

- Concentrate for one day on your emotional responses to different situations: pride, fear, anger, dread, sadness, elation, humility. Ask yourself, "What information is this emotion giving me about myself?" Then pray and surrender yourself to God while asking Him to strengthen and, if necessary, to heal you.

Father, this spiritual discipline of prayer has been the chief business of Your great saints throughout the ages. Lord, we pray that You would make it our chief business too. We want to understand that prayer is a conversation with You—back and forth—and that by this conversation, a precious salvation also becomes a close relationship. Father, please encourage me to sit regularly with You in Your school of prayer. Give me the conviction that prayer is the most powerful and efficient investment of time. Also, help each of us to set prayer as our first disposition. Whatever we encounter, good or bad, may our automatic response be to pray—to talk it out with You. We ask this in the name and the power of Jesus. Amen.

A Review of the Big Ideas

🜄 The risk of not praying is not only that you may not get what you want, but that you get what you don't want.

🜄 Men who pray a lot (1) spend time in the "school of prayer"; (2) come to see prayer as the most powerful and efficient use of their time; and (3) make prayer their first disposition.

🜄 We all have moments when life just doesn't work. In those moments we must be confident that prayer is the most powerful and efficient use of time.

🜄 If you really want to pray regularly, you'll find a way.

🜄 Prayer is a conversation intended to turn your salvation into a close communion and intimate relationship with our Lord and Savior Jesus Christ.

Discussion Questions

1. Look up these passages and record what they tell you about prayer:

> Matthew 6:5–15, 25–34
>
> Mark 11:20–26
>
> Luke 11:1–13
>
> John 14:1–14

2. Of the passages listed above, write one truth that you found surprising, and one way you can apply it to your prayer journey.

3. This chapter lists three characteristics of a praying man. What are they?

4. Based on that list, would you say you are a praying man? Why or why not?

5. If you said you are not, do you have the desire to correct that? If so, what specific steps are you going to take to pursue prayer as a spiritual discipline?

Additional Resources

With Christ in the School Prayer, by Andrew Murray

Celebration of Discipline, by Richard Foster (includes a very good chapter on intercessory prayer)

Praying Hyde, by Francis McGraw (a biography of a prayer warrior)

Letters to Malcolm Chiefly on Prayer, by C.S. Lewis

God in the Dock, by C.S. Lewis (has an excellent article called "Work and Prayer")

A MAN AND WORSHIP

PREVIEW

In this chapter we will define worship, discovering that you can worship many things besides God, but those things will never satisfy. We'll:

- **Profile three kinds of men who face – their own temptations,**

- **Learn how each can find strength and fulfillment through worshiping God.**

- **Understand how worship is more than an event or an activity—it's a lifestyle of submission to God.**

Formula One towers as the pinnacle of automobile racing. Ferrari, for example, invests an estimated $300 million annually to compete at this level. Ferrari's former chief driver, Michael Schumacher, the most successful driver in history, has ranked as the highest paid athlete in the world. Some years Schumacher has won as many as 75 percent of the races, even though competing against twenty-one other world-class drivers.

I'm a Formula One fan. As you know, anyone who develops an interest like this tends to go deeper and deeper into it. One afternoon a man doing some work in my home mentioned that he and his friend had a Formula One video game. I decided to go to an electronics store to check it out.

The next thing I knew, I was trying to explain to my wife why I had a trunk full of electronic toys. "Since I have a ministry and write books," I said in jest, "I need to understand the culture." But the reality is, I love speed and competition.

After hooking up on our Play Station 2 the current version of the Formula One racing game, "F1 2002," I selected Michael Schumacher's car. Soon I was on a virtual straightaway, going more than 180 miles an hour. The whole world disappeared. There were no distractions. I was focused. I was winning . . . and then my wife opened the door and said, "Our son John is on the phone."

Do you have any idea how hard it is to control a Formula One car going 180 miles per hour once you've lost your context? I spun out of control back and forth in every direction, then careened into the guardrail, coming to an abrupt halt. My son comes first.

What Is Worship?

The person who comes to worship is to become as absorbed in communion with God as I was absorbed in that video game. First and foremost, worship means to block out all distractions—even if only for a few moments—and have a 100 percent connection with God. But worship also occurs 24-7; it's daily living in the overflow of those special moments with God. For example, as we will explain further, even our work can be an act of worship.

In the Old Testament, the Hebrew word for *worship* means "to bow down or to prostrate yourself." In the New Testament, the Greek word for worship means "to kiss, the way a dog licks its master's hand."

J. I. Packer, a modern-day Puritan, said in *A Quest for Godliness*, "What is worship? It is essentially doxology, a giving of glory, praise, honor, and homage to God. In the broadest sense of the word, all true piety is worship. 'Godliness is a worship.'"[1] Webster's dictionary calls *worship* "an extravagant respect or admiration for or devotion to an object of esteem." Christians offer this devotion to our God. Says Packer, worship is "all our direct communion with God: invocation, adoration, meditation, faith, praise, prayer and the receiving of instruction from his word, both in public and in private."[2]

Worshiping God

Even as Christians, it is possible to worship someone (or something) other than God. The great colonial preacher Jonathan Edwards observed that man is always worshiping something, whether it's an amusement or an individual or an idol.

Scripture recognizes this tendency too, warning about the futility of worshiping anyone or anything other than God. The first of the Ten Commandments is "You shall have no other gods before me" (Exodus 20:3). The commandment goes on to forbid anyone to create an object for the purpose of worshiping it. God desires our worship, but He wants it to be our response to Him alone.

During a conversation with a Samaritan woman, Jesus declared, "A time is coming and has now come when the true worshipers will worship the Father in spirit and truth, for they are the kind of worshipers the Father seeks. God is spirit and his worshipers must worship in spirit and truth" (John 4:23–24).

God wants His disciples to be worshipers. So it's important that we understand what makes worship different from other spiritual disciplines.

What happens when we worship? The creature, keenly aware of his "creatureliness," comes into the presence of the one true Holy Father and communes with Him. The experience calls us to exalt, to revere, and to praise. In this spiritual discipline we prostrate ourselves before our Holy God.

For me, worshiping God means I'm so caught up in Him that, as already said, it's like going 180 miles an hour down a straightaway. I'm completely oblivious to everything around me. I'm completely absorbed in the person, the Godhead, the Trinity—the Father, the Son, and the Holy Spirit.

Our worship influences our relationship with Him, but it also influences our relationship with everything else. Consider the prophet Isaiah. In Isaiah 6 we find the prophet in the temple, implying that he was worshiping. As he was worshiping he saw God. He came face-to-face with the holy God, and became keenly aware of who he was. He saw himself as a man who needed the cleansing only God could provide. So he repented and, once accomplished, his life purpose became clear to him. Worship can provide that kind of clarity.

Why Should We Worship?

Doug Coupland, who wrote *Generation X* and popularized the term *GenX*, also wrote a book called *Life After God*. Our almost insatiable appetite for distraction really culminates in a man like Coupland, who represents an entire generation of Western young people. Let me quote from the dustcover of *Life After God*:

> As suburban children we floated at night in swimming pools the temperature of blood, pools the color of earth as seen from outer space. You are the first generation raised without religion. What happens if we are raised without religion or belief? As we grow older the beauty and enchantment of the world tempers our souls. We are all living creatures with strong religious impulses, yet where do these impulses flow in a world of malls, TV, Kraft dinners and jets? How do we cope with loneliness? How do we deal with anxiety, the clash of relationships? How do we reach the quiet, safe layer of our lives?

Coupland tells many such stories in the book, but on the next to last page he writes this conclusion:

> Now—here is my secret: I tell it to you with an openness of heart that I doubt I shall ever achieve again, so I pray that you are in a quiet room as you hear these words. My secret is that I need God—that I am sick and can no longer make it alone. I need God to help me give, because I no longer seem to be capable of giving; to help me be kind, as I no longer seem capable of kindness; to help me love, as I seem beyond being able to love.[3]

We live in a world awash with amusements. Let me say up front: Amusements are fun, and for the most part they're good. We sometimes need distractions. But eventually we notice a deeper hunger in our souls that cannot be satisfied by mere amusements. Entertainments can lead the soul into a longing, but we don't always understand what, or whom, we desire. Coupland discovered his longing was for God. *Note: I wrote Doug Coupland and sent him a book. He called, we had a wonderful conversation, and, if I understood him correctly, he has become a Christian.*

We can draw two pictures of the process described by Coupland. The first shows a man with a lamp, searching the universe for a God who is hiding. The second shows man eating and making merry, while God sends spokespeople—prophets and preachers—yet the man will not listen.

What does Scripture say? Remember Jesus' conversation with the Samaritan woman? He said God is seeking worshipers. So if God and man don't get together, it's not because He's hiding—it's because we are. We worship because we must.

Three Kinds of Men

Our response to God will depend largely on whether we are hurting, hollow, or happy.

A Hurting Man

Charles is a hurting man. Perhaps he was just minding his own business when he was overtaken by evil. Or perhaps he is suffering from the consequences of his own sins.

Charles didn't think God could fill him up and satisfy him. So he found a woman. Perhaps he made an idol of sex. He believed he had every reason to succumb to this temptation, because his wife had emotionally disconnected from him twenty years ago. There was no warmth in the relationship. Every day for two decades he lived with a woman who gave him nothing. He was emotionally hungry. But instead of finding satisfaction in God, he chose to find it in a relationship with a woman.

In His grace, God will remove all idols. Charles still hurts, but for a different reason. Now he's been found out. He's being chastened and disciplined. What is his greatest need?

A Hollow Man

Dillon feels that life is pointless and meaningless. His situation is a little different from Charles's. For Charles, life isn't working. For Dillon, it's working okay, but so what? Everything is going fine, but it just doesn't seem to matter. He has every reason to be happy, but he isn't.

To Dillon, life is some sort of malicious joke worked out by a cruel puppeteer. His joy has succumbed to the fog of doubt. Rather than challenging the notion of futility, Bruce seeks distraction. He may still go through the motions of Christianity—still attend church, still pray, still read the Bible. But at his core, our hollow man Dillon is saying, "I'm not sure I really believe all this."

A Happy Man

Josh seems content. His career is going well, he's got a great marriage, and his relationship with God is awesome. He has satisfied the three things that every man needs. He has (1) something to give his life to, (2) someone to share it with, and (3) a belief system that gives him a reasonable explanation for why the first two are such a struggle!

Josh still faces his own set of temptations, and the biggest one is the tendency to take the source of his happiness for granted. He may become complacent. Or worse, he may make an idol of success, taking credit for it himself.

A hurting man sees God differently than a hollow man, and a happy man, in turn, views God differently than a hurting or hollow man. A man who worships correctly sees God as He is—as Creator. And he sees himself as he is—a creation. His lifestyle reflects that perspective.

To Give Rather Than "to Win" Worship

The Weight of Glory contains several unpublished messages of C. S. Lewis, compiled by his secretary, Walter Hooper. In the introduction, he commented that Lewis was the most modest person he had ever known. Hooper wrote, "One evening this came up rather naturally. We had been talking about one of our favourite books, . . . and I mentioned how disappointed I sometimes felt when, say, Sir Lancelot went out to deliver a helpless lady from some peril or other. Then, just at that point where you can't admire him enough for selflessness, he explains to someone, as though it was the most natural thing in the world, that [Lancelot] is doing this to 'win worship'—that is, to increase his reputation."[4]

"Without intending any embarrassment," Hooper added, "I asked Lewis if he was ever aware of the fact that regardless of his intentions he was 'winning worship' from his books. He said in a low, still voice, and with the deepest and most complete humility I've ever observed in anyone, 'One cannot be too careful *not* to think about it.' The house, the garden, the whole universe seemed hushed for a moment, and then we began talking again."[5]

Pursuing the Discipline of Worship

Lewis was aware that, like Lancelot, he must be careful not to seek worship. Similarly, in my ministry, I've never spoken to an audience that did not include men like Charles, Dillon, and Josh. Some are hurting. Some are hollow. Some are happy. Everybody falls into at least one category—perhaps more than one, for various reasons. They bring different problems, but they find solutions in the same way, through worship of God alone.

The soul's deepest hunger is to worship its Creator. That's how a hurting man gets healed. That's how a hollow man receives satisfaction. And that's how a happy man stays happy.

We all have deep longings for love, for meaning, for happiness. Yet we won't find those things by pursuing them, because they distract us from facing our ultimate craving. The basic cry of our souls is for worship. Nothing else will fill that void.

Look at Psalm 42, beginning with verse 1. This passage says, "As the deer pants for streams of water, so my soul pants for you, O God. My soul thirsts for God, for the living God. When can I go and meet with God?"

Verses 5–8 says, "Why are you downcast, O my soul? Why so disturbed within me? Put your hope in God, for I will yet praise him, my Savior and my God. My soul is downcast within me; therefore I will remember you from the land of Jordan, the heights of Hermon. Deep calls to deep in the roar of your waterfalls; all your waves and breakers have swept over me." Clearly, this passage pictures a man whose deepest desire is to worship God.

Suggestions for Pursuing Worship

How do you do this? Psalm 95 gives a pretty clear picture of worship. It says, "Come, let us sing for joy to the LORD; let us shout aloud to the Rock of our salvation. Let us come before him with thanksgiving and extol him with music and song" (verses 1–2). Go back through those verses and circle all the verbs and their modifiers. You'll see worship can be expressed as we "sing for joy," or "shout aloud," or "come with thanksgiving," or "extol him with music."

To pursue the discipline of worship, we can sing. We can declare—shout aloud—His worth. We can appear prayerfully before Him and others with thankful hearts—an attitude of gratefulness. We can let great music turn our hearts and minds toward Him.

Suggested Spiritual Exercises

Here are ten practical suggestions for a richer worship life. Some of these, no doubt, you already do. Some of these may not ring your bell at all. Remember, this is not a magical list of things you can do to worship God, but they are some things that will give you more of a continuous or daily type of worship experience and, therefore, daily renewal. The list is by no means exhaustive.

1. Preparation

I asked David Delk, president of Man in the Mirror, "What do you think are the most practical things I could suggest to these men?" He astutely observed, "I don't care what else you tell them, but just tell them to take two breaths before they start." This is the idea of preparation. For example, when you're lying in bed before you roll out in the morning, prepare yourself for the day. Turn your thoughts to God and maybe say a prayer. On your way to church on Sundays, before you leave the house, think about what you're going to do. Help your family think about it too!

2. Creation

You could use a lot of different words for this, but this is the idea of contemplating God's creation, His general revelation (amplified in chapter 1). I love to sit out in the backyard before daybreak and look up into the star-saturated sky and just imagine God taking His hand, dipping it into a bowl of liquid light, and flicking His fingers against the curtain of the night.

How do you understand that? I can't. So, instead, I fall down and worship. Contemplating the majesty of creation can lead you to a transcendent moment that leaves you with a deeper sense of awe and reverence of our great God.

3. The Bible

The Bible is where we gain knowledge of the gospel of Jesus Christ, of faith and repentance and obedience, and how we might live our lives. You might consider having a regular place in your home where you go. I know that when I go to that place, I am going to meet with God there because I am going to look into His Word. I am going to study, and I'm going to allow Him to speak to me in private through His Word.

4. Prayer

There are all kinds of ways to pray. There are set prayers, and there are spontaneous prayers. I would encourage you to have a running conversation with God. Most people have a running conversation with themselves. "I wonder whether I should go to that party tonight? I wonder whether I should buy this product from that person? I wonder whom I should call for my next sales presentation. I wonder, I wonder, I wonder . . . " Maybe you could turn those thoughts into prayers and have a running conversation with God—a form of continuous worship that could lead to continuous renewal, not to mention continuous guidance.

5. Books

I love books. In his book *The Reformed Pastor,* Richard Baxter wrote in 1656, "See that in every family there are some useful, moving books besides the Bible. If they have none, persuade them to buy some. If they be not able to buy them, give them some if you can. If you are not able yourself, get some gentlemen or other rich persons that are ready to do good works to do it and engage them to read them at night when they have leisure and, especially, on the Lord's day."[6] If you want to have new thoughts about God, you can do that by reading the Bible, but also by reading good Christian literature. I have always been amazed at how a man will get hold of a book, and then God will use the book to get hold of the man.

6. Music

Another window into worship is through music. Many days I pop a CD of worship music into my car's CD player. Almost instantly, I find myself in a state of worship as I drive along. Instant worship leads to instant renewal. So whether you're a salesman between appointments, a lawyer on your way to a deposition, or a computer programmer in your cubicle, put on the headphones and enjoy music that inspires you to worship and praise and adore our great God.

7. Journaling

Experiment with jotting down your thoughts. How about a pencil or a pen? Me, I like typing into my computer. I keep an annual journal, but I don't have any pattern, rhyme, or reason to it. But whenever I have a thought that I think is worth recording, I put it in my journal, and it helps me sort out my thinking. A lot of times we have thoughts and we lose them completely—they're gone forever. So writing them down is a great way of capturing our worshipful thoughts.

8. Public Worship (Church)

Worshiping together in community makes God more tangible. Caring about brothers and sisters in Christ honors God. Richard Foster, in his book *Celebration of Discipline,* has a chapter on the discipline of worship. One thing he suggests, and I've been doing it ever since, is to arrive at church, look around, and find people who have drooped shoulders and, under the leading of the Spirit, pray for them. I pray for the pastor; I pray for the worshipers; I pray for the experience. It's interesting how much I get up for worship by helping others get up for worship.

9. Family Worship

If you are married, don't neglect leading your wife and children into a deeper holiness and experience of worshiping God. Gather your family in the morning to pray for the day. Take five minutes and share how you saw God work the day before. Ask everyone for prayer requests. Dedicate the day to His glory and praise. When you gather for meals, be sure to ask God's blessing and offer thanks. It's a wonderful example, and certainly captures the Greek concept of worship—"to kiss, the way a dog licks its master's hand."

10. Work

Broadcaster Roy Firestone once interviewed a seven-foot tall, 260-pound specimen of pure muscle and athleticism, a man who had led his team to back-to-back championships and had been named an all-star twelve times and one of the best big men in the history of the National Basketball Association. "Your teammates tell me that every time you hit the hardwood you give 110 percent," Firestone said. "They say that you'll go out and practice and shoot hook shots for hours and hours and hours. They tell me that you will run wind sprints until you literally cannot walk anymore. They say that during a scrimmage that you will go for loose balls like it's the NBA finals. Why? You're one of the best there has ever been in this game. Why don't you just lie back and take it easy?"

He said, "Roy, you need to know something. When I go out onto the hardwood, I'm not going to work. I'm going to worship. How would I dare to not give back to God what He has given to me with joy and thanksgiving? No, I don't go to work. I go to worship."

His name is Hakeem Olajuwan. He's a Muslim. He's not a Christian, and yet God in His providence has given him the insight that our work is meant to be an act of worship.

Being Overwhelmed by God's Greatness

The bottom line is this: Worship is a personal expression of being overwhelmed by God's goodness and greatness. Worship includes any activity that enhances or expresses your understanding of God's supremacy and your submission to Him. Your communication of that concept is limited only by your creativity. You can do it any way you want. You can do it in public or in private.

I recommend you worship God every day. Make it a habit. Go through your day seeking opportunities to worship God, to praise Him, to exalt Him, to revere Him. Practice worshiping Him about everything—every family argument, every late-paying customer, every complaining employee, every person you see and greet on a daily basis. Worship can be a scary word, yet it's a relatively simple thing to do. Just let your soul commune with God in a greater way every day.

Lord, when things are going really well, it's easy to lose our focus on worshiping You, when that should be the very cause of worship. Lord, when we feel hollow and think life is pointless, the way out of that must certainly be to come into Your presence and commune with You. No matter what our circumstances, the way we satisfy the soul's deepest hunger is always the same—we must learn to worship our Creator. Lord, I'm not sure what You want to do in our lives, but I know You want to do something. So I pray You'd help

each of us respond to Your promptings. Help each of us to continue
to grow as worshipers of You, the one true God. In Christ's name.
Amen.

Here is a summary of the ten practical worship suggestions. In the space provided, put a "1" for "very present," a "2" for "somewhat present," and a "3" for "not present."

Now circle the suggestions you find yourself most interested in pursuing.

___ **Preparation**   ___ **Music**

___ **Creation**   ___ **Journaling**

___ **The Bible**   ___ **Public Worship**

___ **Prayer**   ___ **Family Worship**

___ **Books**   ___ **Work**

A Review of the Big Ideas

ᶜ In the Old Testament, the Hebrew word for worship means "to bow down or to prostrate yourself."

ᶜ In the New Testament, the Greek word for worship means "to kiss, the way a dog licks its master's hand."

ᶜ Our response to Him will depend largely on whether we are hurting, hollow, or happy.

ᶜ A man who worships correctly sees God as He is—as Creator of the universe. And he sees himself as he is—as a creation.

ᶜ The bottom line is, worship is a personal expression of being overwhelmed by God's goodness and greatness.

ᶜ Worship can be a scary word, yet it's a relatively simple thing to do. Just let your soul commune with God in a greater way every day.

Discussion Questions

1. Are you a hurting man, a hollow man, or a happy man? How does that affect your ability to worship?

2. We tend to define worship in terms of what happens on Sunday at church. But that's too narrow of a definition. Look up Romans 12:1–2. What does that tell you about worship as a lifestyle?

3. Of the ten practical suggestions mentioned, which would you most like to explore further?

4. Give an example of something you can do today or tomorrow as an act of worship. What is your plan?

Additional Resources

I have created a Web site location where you can obtain additional resources. At www.maninthemirror.org/spiritual disciplines you will find a free message, "A Man Created to Worship," from the Biblical Manhood series on video or audio that you can stream or download. Go to this link and click on message 9. Enjoy enjoy two free, downloadable, printable articles on sensing the presence of God.

5

A MAN AND THE SABBATH

PREVIEW

In this chapter, we will answer three questions related to the Sabbath:

- **What is the meaning of Sabbath?**
- **Is Sabbath simply a legalistic requirement?**
- **Is Sabbath for today or is it just an Old Testament idea?**

John glanced at his watch. This meeting was running a lot longer than he anticipated. He ran his finger around his collar, loosening it a bit as he eyed in irritation the people sitting on his left and right. He needed to leave. He had a string of deadlines fast approaching. How on earth was he going to finish everything?

John had worked at least ten hours per day for nine straight days. He was still "tying up loose ends." One more day, and he should have everything covered. He tapped his finger on the conference room table and sat on the edge of his seat. Finally the team leader said, "Okay. Meeting adjourned."

John hastily exited the room and headed toward his office. "Your wife is on line two," his assistant reported as he walked briskly past her desk.

"Hi, what do you want?" he growled as he picked up the phone.

"Just wondered if you'll be home for dinner."

"Doesn't look like it," he said.

"But that's a whole week now." His wife sighed. "The kids are starting to forget what you look like."

"Can't help it," he snarled. "I've gotta go."

John checked his e-mail. Two messages from the operations department—requests for more specific information about an order he wanted them to place for him. "These people are so stupid," he muttered. "Why can't people figure it out for themselves?"

John is sailing into dangerous water. Let's coin a new term: He's suffering from what we might call *rest-interval dysfunction*. His life is out of balance, and he needs to take a break. He needs a Sabbath.

What Is Sabbath?

The word *Sabbath* literally means "to cease activity or to rest." We get our word *sabbatical* from this root. Through the ages controversy has swirled around the Sabbath commandment, as theologians and would-be theologians have discussed whether it relates to a specific day of the week, and whether specific activities are allowed while others are outlawed. But for the purpose of this chapter, I simply want to make this point: We all have a responsibility, and also a right or privilege, to enjoy regular intervals of rest.

Check out what the Bible says in Deuteronomy 5:12–15. This portion is right in the middle of the recording of the Ten Commandments—in fact, it's the fourth commandment, and it's the longest of the ten. It says:

> Observe the Sabbath day by keeping it holy, as the LORD your God has commanded you. Six days you shall labor and do all your work, but the seventh day is a Sabbath to the LORD your God. On it you shall not do any work, neither you, nor your son or daughter, nor your manservant or maidservant, nor your ox, your donkey or any of your animals, nor the alien within your gates, so that your manservant and maidservant may rest, as you do. Remember that you were slaves in Egypt and that

the LORD your God brought you out of there with a mighty hand and an outstretched arm. Therefore the LORD your God has commanded you to observe the Sabbath day.

Biblically, the Sabbath has purpose. Certainly it's for resting and refueling. But it's also for remembering. It's a day that is set apart. We don't work. We don't require others to work. That's the Old Testament Sabbath.

Compare that passage from Deuteronomy with this one from Exodus 23:12, which says, "Six days do your work, but on the seventh day do not work, so that your ox and your donkey may rest and the slave born in your household, and the alien as well, may be refreshed."

From these two passages we see that the Sabbath is a beautiful gift from God to His children. God has made it legal for us to set apart one day a week for rest.

The story is told about English street merchants who claimed that when they rested their donkeys one day a week, they could carry their loads thirty miles per day. But when they drove their donkeys every day of the week, they only averaged fifteen miles per day—and they looked terrible! By resting their donkeys one day a week they not only nearly doubled the output, but the donkeys were healthy and happy. No doubt the same is true for humans.

Why Should We Honor the Sabbath as a Spiritual Discipline?

For some of us twenty-first-century hard-chargers, rest really requires an act of discipline. It's not our natural response. We're more comfortable working and involved in activity. Yet God thought it was important enough to make it one of His crucial mandates. Why should we pay attention to that? I see at least four reasons to practice the discipline of the Sabbath:

1. *The Sabbath is integral to orthodox Christianity*. It is included in the Ten Commandments—arguably the most important pieces of legislation ever recorded. They help form the foundation for Western culture.

2. *The Sabbath expresses our trust in God's provision.* Our obedience communicates that our faith is in God—not in ourselves. By resting we say, "I believe God will take care of me. I don't always have to be scrambling. I can trust Him."

3. *The Sabbath protects us from ourselves.* Many years ago it was said that, when Frenchmen in Paris stopped observing the Sabbath, suicide rates increased. During that time, the suicide rate in Paris reportedly became the highest of any city in the Christianized world. Constant work will wear us down, put us on edge, and make us unbalanced.

4. *The Sabbath is badly misunderstood, often abused, and frequently neglected.* Whether it's mowing, shopping, or just doing lots of chores, many people don't relax on the weekends. Many men who do relax leave God out of this day of recreation. They often ignore their families. One student trying to draw attention to the neglect of the Sabbath in our generation wrote a satirical tract called "I believe in all nine of the Ten Commandments." The title might make you smile, but take a moment to really think about the implications.

Suppose you don't acknowledge God's provision of Sabbath. Suppose you just keep working. Or when you're not working, you're completely addicted to your hobbies or sports, or sit vegetating in front of ESPN. You're doing "manly things" with other men. There's nothing wrong with those activities—but what if that's all you do, all the time?

What happens to your family relationships? They grow stone cold and disintegrate. That will happen in your natural family, and it will happen in your spiritual family.

Here's the bottom line: A man who doesn't honor the Sabbath, who doesn't invest any time celebrating his place in God's family, will succumb to stress. He will become spiritually isolated from God and from other people. He will make poor decisions. And the church will become weaker because of his absence.

Admittedly, it's not always easy to refuse to work one day out of every seven. That's why it's a discipline—something you work into your lifestyle through training. God legalized a day of rest. If you work an occasional

Sunday, it's okay, but if every Sunday night you compulsively take an hour or two to plan out your week, you may want to reexamine your commitment to keeping the Sabbath. If you feel you can't get by without working on the Sabbath, you may want to ask yourself, "Am I trusting God? If not, what am I afraid of?"

Living Out a Commitment to the Sabbath

In the Beginning . . .

Some people think the Sabbath ideal is a holdover from the Old Testament. They probably never knew that the Sabbath precedes the giving of the Law. Genesis 2:2 tells us God incorporated Sabbath into creation, when He worked six days and then "on the seventh day he rested."

God originated the idea of a seven-day week, with one day set aside for rest. The seven-day cycle doesn't correspond to anything else—not the lunar cycle, nor any cycle of stars. It grows from the creation ordinance.

God's Moral Law

Furthermore, the New Testament did not do away with all Old Testament law. Certainly, Colossians 2:14 tells us Jesus "canceled the written code." It says He "took it away, nailing it to the cross." In context, though, let's consider that the Old Testament includes three kinds of law:

1. *Ceremonial law*, made up of rituals.

2. *Judicial law*, made up of rules and consequences governing personal and social behavior

3. *Moral law*, made up of injunctions that always have been and always will be right. The Ten Commandments, including the injunction related to Sabbath, fall into this final category. Ceremonial and judicial laws were repealed through Christ's life, death, and resurrection. But God's moral law remains. These principles are repeated throughout the New Testament, because they explain and reflect God's character.

Jesus taught extensively on the moral law, including the Sabbath. In Mark 2:28, for instance, He said, "The Son of Man is Lord even of the Sabbath." That makes it very much a part of the New Testament.

So the Sabbath principle applies to our contemporary world. Yet even among those who accept that view, people regard Sunday, or the Sabbath, from different perspectives. Some see it as a family day. Others think of it as "game day" for whatever sport is currently in season. Some see it as fun day, set aside for personal or family recreation. Still others think of Sunday as "my day"—every other day belongs to my creditors, but Sunday is my day, and I don't want anybody to interfere with it. These people get up on Sunday, kick back, have a third cup of coffee, read the newspaper, and go to church if they feel like it.

The Lord's Day

But the Bible says it's the Lord's Day. God is not so interested in external behavior, except as it reveals what's going on in the heart. So think about how you spend your Sabbaths. Are you so tired on Monday that you can barely function? If so, you have rest-interval dysfunction. If you go so hard on Sunday that you are weary on Monday, can you claim to be honoring the Sabbath?

People also hold various views about what types of activities are permissible on Sundays (the day most people consider the Sabbath). When my children were growing up, we went out to dinner every Sunday night. It was a way to pull the family together at the end of the weekend, and we thought we were keeping the Sabbath.

Then my daughter went to work for a Christian ministry. One night she called, and we weren't home to answer. So when we finally caught up with each other, she asked where we had been. We had just returned from our Sunday night dinner. She said she been studying about the Sabbath, and she wasn't sure she wanted to eat out any more on Sundays. She said it was a matter of her own personal conscience, because it forced other people to work.

I argued, "They're going to be working anyway, so why not go?"

She replied, "Yeah, I know. But it bothers my conscience that I'm contributing to them having to work. I'm not going out to eat anymore on Sunday."

That started working on me. The simple truth is, if you look at the Ten Commandments from a certain perspective, you come up with a long list of little dos and don'ts. If you look at it from Christ's perspective, you understand that Jesus is interested in your attitude. He gives great freedom and liberty.

So occasionally my wife and I still go out to eat on Sundays, but it's no longer our habit. It's our choice. Other people may choose to eat out on Sundays. That's okay too. I see no set of "rules." The main thing about the Sabbath is your attitude. Are you approaching it the way God intended?

By the way, my daughter went on to seminary to earn degrees in theological studies and counseling. When I asked her for permission to use this story she said, "You know, I'm actually more where you are on the Sabbath since going to seminary." Again, it's about not abusing our freedom.

If you work at physical labor all week, then perhaps Sunday is a good day to take a nap. If you have a sedentary job, you may want to exercise in the afternoon. That can be a perfectly acceptable way to set apart the day. The key is balance.

In my book *Discipleship for the Man in the Mirror*, I have a chart. It looks like this:

Law   **Liberty**   **License**

Clearly, law and license are inappropriate extremes. Liberty is the place of balance. The proper biblical response is to end up somewhere near the middle with the liberty that comes through grace and brings freedom.

Suggestions for Pursuing The Discipline of the Sabbath Rest

Our overall goal when it comes to honoring the Sabbath is to apply spiritual wisdom and find the place of liberty. If you have a little rest-interval dysfunction, consider these suggestions.

Starting the Day with the Father

Remember the Sabbath a day God set aside for rest, and He cares about our hearts. With that in mind, here's what a day of rest might look like: Wake up at the normal time, but don't roll out of bed right away. Lie in bed for an extra fifteen or twenty minutes and pray. Thank God for the Sabbath and think about this as a special day in God's economy. Thank God for making it legal for us to set it aside for rest.

Then consider the reason for a day of rest—God wants it to be holy. He wants us to remember. He wants us to worship. He wants to have fellowship with us. The Sabbath is about spending time with God.

When you rise from bed, you may have a time of personal devotions. This is a good time to review the previous week and thank God for His protection and provision. I remember a few things I didn't get finished, and I pray about them too. Then I pray through the week to come. Ask God to watch over you, to give you favor and to bless you, to guide you, to give you wisdom—and wisdom to your loved ones too!

Next, you may set aside the money you will give to God's work—a tithe. Look at how much money came into the household the past week and figure how much you're going to give. Before you leave for church, write out the check; then pray and offer to God a sacrifice of praise.

When you enter church, think about the needs of those around you. Even before I leave for church, I think about brothers and sisters in the fellowship who are hurting. When I get to church, I might look around for somebody with drooped shoulders, or someone who's standing off in the corner with nobody to talk to. I pray for those people. I might go over and engage someone in conversation.

Be sure to worship God as you sing. When fellow believers sing the music in church, I let go. I worship God. I don't worry about what people around me are thinking of my singing. I'm singing to Jesus, and to my Father, through the Holy Spirit. When church is over, I enjoy a little fellowship with some people.

Relax the Rest of the Day

Enjoy your lunch; you have time today. As I said, you can either eat at home or out, depending on how God leads you.

Depending on how I feel after that, I may want to take a nap, or watch sports on TV. I read and study all week, so on Sundays, I like to zone out. Then, toward evening, my wife and I have dinner at home together, and we spend some time talking about what's going on in our lives. Go to bed at a reasonable time so you will be ready for Monday. Usually I go to bed early so I don't wake up with rest-interval dysfunction on Monday morning.

That's how I spend most Sundays, and for the most part, I think I've found a balance between law and license. However, I also race a sports car, so about one weekend per month I wake up at a race track, but I still find time to worship and pray. We sometimes have a chapel service at the track. I've found liberty. You can find it too—but it will require discipline until it becomes habit.

Suggested Spiritual Exercises

- Prepare for church in a different way. Possibly include your family.

- Spend some amount of time in Sabbath every day. You are probably already doing this—a quiet cup of coffee in the morning, debriefing your day with your spouse, or taking a midday nap. It may be as simple as thinking differently about something you are already doing.

Father, the Sabbath is a beautiful gift. You have given us the Sabbath as a legal right. It's also a responsibility. Please give each of us the wisdom to see how keeping the Sabbath will affect us Monday morning and throughout the week. For those who have rest-interval dysfunction, help us look at our own hearts to see if the way we "do" Sabbath is contributing to that problem. For those who are legalists, help us to view the Sabbath in liberty; and for those who have chosen to ignore the Sabbath, help us think righteously and reach that freedom that comes through Your liberty. We pray this prayer in the power and name of Jesus. Amen.

A Review of the Big Ideas

⅄ God has made it legal for us to set apart one day a week for rest.

⅄ We all have a responsibility, and also a right or privilege, to enjoy regular intervals of rest.

⅄ A man who doesn't honor the Sabbath, who doesn't invest any time celebrating his place in God's family, will succumb to stress.

⅄ God originated the idea of a seven-day week, with one day set aside for rest.

⅄ If you work at physical labor all week, then perhaps Sunday is a good day to take a nap.

⅄ I thank God for the Sabbath, and I think about this as a special day in God's economy.

Discussion Questions

1. Describe a memorable Sabbath. What made it so special?

2. Why did God set apart a day of rest according to Exodus 23:12 and Deuteronomy 5:12–15?

3. Is the Sabbath for today? Look up Matthew 5:17–19: What kind of law is Jesus talking about (ceremonial, judicial, moral)? Look up Mark 2:28: What is the relationship between Jesus and the Sabbath? Is there any biblical warrant to reduce the Ten Commandments to nine? What are the implications for you?

4. What happens when men don't "set apart" a day as the Sabbath and keep it holy? What happens when men think of Sunday (or Saturday) as *my day, work day, play day, game day,* or even *family day?*

5. The Sabbath is a beautiful gift from God to His children. Why not make a specific plan to receive this Sunday as a beautiful gift for you and your family?

6

A MAN AND FELLOWSHIP

PREVIEW

In this chapter, we will discuss why we need relationships with other believers, and specifically, why we need to pursue small-group fellowship. We'll:

- **Examine our need for encouragement and exhortation.**
- **Look at settings where we can "fill each others' gaps" as members of the Christian body.**

In some ways, men are like redwood trees. Redwoods grow for millennia—some are two thousand years old. They reach as high as 350 feet. Yet their roots generally run only six to ten feet below the surface. How do these top-heavy monsters stand the tests of storms and high winds? They grow close together, and they intermingle their roots. In essence, they stand strong because they stand together.

In today's world, men often have an independent "go-it-alone" mentality. Yet, like redwoods, we will find it's easier to stand strong when we stand together. Many spiritual disciplines require solitude, but that doesn't mean it's always good to be alone.

When we make a conscious, intentional effort to foster relationships with other men who also are trying to follow Jesus wholeheartedly, we are engaged in the spiritual discipline of fellowship. Men who open themselves honestly to other like-minded men find sustenance and encouragement in life's backbreaking storms. It's more than "misery loves company." It's more like: I know God is real because I can see Him in you.

What Is Fellowship?

Some men may balk at the term *fellowship*. It may not seem like a masculine need. So let's look at some synonyms—*friendship*, *partnership*, *gathering*, *camaraderie*, *building and encouraging relationships*, *brotherhood*, *hanging out*, and *getting together*. Suddenly it doesn't sound so bad.

A Deep Inner Need

The need for relationship is deeply rooted in all of us. Genesis 2 says that before God created Eve, He put Adam in a garden and gave him responsibility to care for it. He gave Adam certain instructions. Then God made a comment: "It is not good for the man to be alone" (Genesis 2:18). We know God ended up creating Eve as a helper and companion. And certainly, for those of us who are married, our closest earthly relationship should be with our wives. Our need for relationships also extends beyond marriage. For example, Hebrews 10:25 says, "Let us not give up meeting together, as some are in the habit of doing, but let us encourage one another" (more on this text later). Going a step further, Proverbs 18:24 says, "There is a friend who sticks closer than a brother." The bottom line is, God did not intend for any man to fight life's challenges by himself. We need one another.

Scripture builds on this theme when it compares the church to a human body. First Corinthians 12:12 says, "The body is a unit, though it is made up of many parts; and though all its parts are many, they form one body."

The word *body* in Greek is used many different ways, but here it basically means *community*. This passage says the community is a unit, although it is made up of many parts. Any assembly of Christians is a gathering of "the body." The next verse says we're all baptized by one spirit into one body, regardless of our ethnicity or our socioeconomic status.

We are one body with many different parts, and we need one another to function effectively. You'll see that in verses 15–20, which says,

If the foot should say, "Because I am not a hand, I do not belong to the body," it would not for that reason cease to be part of the body. And if the ear should say, "Because I am not an eye, I do not belong to the body," it would not for that reason cease to be part of the body. If the whole body were an eye, where would the sense of hearing be? If the whole body were an ear, where would the sense of smell be? But in fact God has arranged the parts in the body, every one of them, just as he wanted us to be. If they were all one part, where would the body be? As it is, there are many parts, but one body.

We can certainly see the wisdom of this passage in the physical realm. Would you really want your body to be nothing but a great big ear? You might be able to hear someone whispering from a mile away. But you'd never see a baby smile. You'd never taste an Italian sausage sandwich. You'd never smell fresh cinnamon rolls. You'd never be able to walk down the hall. You'd never pet your dog.

Needing One Another to Survive

Now, let's apply this idea to the Christian body. Did you ever wonder, "Why can't I be a man with a servant heart like Jim?" Or "Why don't I encourage people like Bill?" Or "When they ask for volunteers to set up the tables, why do I go the other way, while Stefan makes a beeline over there?" Well we all have different parts to play in this body. God designed us that way on purpose, so that we need one another to survive as a body.

Let's pick up that passage again in verse 21, which says, "The eye cannot say to the hand, 'I don't need you!' And the head cannot say to the feet, 'I don't need you!'" Do you see where this is going? The passage goes on to say, "Those parts of the body that seem to be weaker are indispensable" (verse 22). If you don't believe it's true, try to walk without a little toe. Or try turning a doorknob without a pinky finger.

The apostle Paul goes on to discuss how "less honorable" parts end up being treated with special honor. And he explains how modesty causes us to cover up certain parts, while others need no special treatment. Then he writes, "God has combined the members of the body and has given greater honor to the parts that lacked it, so that there should be no division in the body, but that its parts should have equal concern for each other. If one part suffers, every part suffers with it; if one part is honored, every part rejoices with it" (verses 24–26).

That's supposed to happen through fellowship. God did not intend for any of us to live out our Christianity as "lone rangers." When we live in relationship with other believers, we accept our place in the body. The big picture is: I need you and you need me.

Why Should We Pursue Fellowship as a Spiritual Discipline?

In His wisdom God has not given any of us everything we need to follow Him successfully. Instead He chose to give us one another. I have gaps, and you have gaps—but in God's plan, we fill one another's gaps. That's the cosmic order.

Several years ago a friend named Isaac said he called his elderly mother every single day. I remember thinking, *I could never do that.* Then my mother fell sick with cancer, and I began calling her every day. She passed away, and my dad was so lonely. He missed her. Why? Because in His wisdom, God does not give any of us everything we need. Instead He chose to give us one another. So I started calling my dad every day.

None of us is a whole body. We're just parts, but we are indispensable parts of one another. Together we're a body. We need one another. We fill one anothers' gaps.

My friend Tom Skinner (now with the Lord) used to say, "The most powerful force in the world is a relationship." And Christian relationships are unique, because they are built on the foundation of Christian love. We have a special bond that breeds a special fellowship that crosses traditional barriers. You know what it's like to travel—to be in another city or on an airplane or in a taxi, and you try to strike up a conversation with somebody, but there is a distance between you. If you're a believer, and you find out the other person also is a Christian, what happens? Instant fellowship! You have a connection, because your part links with his part, and the parts become a whole.

Living Out a Commitment to Fellowship

Obviously, we've all experienced the lower levels of fellowship—a ball team, a fraternity, or even a gang. But let's take a look at another Scripture passage to see what biblical fellowship should look like. Hebrews 10:24 says, "And let us consider how we may spur one another on toward love and good deeds." *Spur on* can also mean "provoke, challenge or inspire." The Greek word could mean "to stimulate" another person to love and good deeds.

Sometimes that kind of challenge is difficult to face. We don't like to admit that we aren't doing everything right. At some point, probably all of us withdraw. We say, "I'm not part of that body. I am a free agent. I do my own thing." If we do that long enough, we will wither up into a little pile of dust, because we need one another.

So the next verse in this passage says, "Let us not give up meeting together, as some are in the habit of doing, but let us encourage one another—and all the more as you see the Day approaching."

The bottom line from Hebrews 10:24–25 is that Christian fellowship is designed to spur us on. God's plan is that we will *exhort* one another and *encourage* one another.

1. We exhort one another.

A few years ago I was talking with a man who attended one of my Bible studies. I found out he had been out of work for quite a while. We spent a half hour on the phone talking about different options. About midway through the conversation I discovered that, in his discouragement, he was sleeping in. He wasn't going to interviews. He was not aggressively pursuing a new position. "Let me ask you," I said, "what do you want here? Do you want a hug or a kick in the pants?"

He admitted, "What I really need is a kick in the pants."

I said, "If you want, I'll hold you accountable. Call me at four o'clock tomorrow afternoon and tell me how many employment interviews you have scheduled."

Sometimes, even when we're down, what we really need is somebody to *exhort* us and spur us on.

Some of you may have recently returned to a bad habit. Or perhaps you are wavering between two options in a moral dilemma. Or, at a really basic level, perhaps you've been fighting with your wife all week. You probably can't solve that problem if you don't open yourself up to someone and admit that you have a "gap." There are exceptions to this rule, but for the most part, you probably don't really need someone to sympathize with you, to say, "Oh, I'm so sorry you yelled at your wife. Oh, poor baby." No, you need a kick in the pants. You need some real-life exhortation. Scripture says that's part of what it means to have biblical fellowship.

2. Encourage one another.

Sometimes we need the kind of confrontation we've just discussed. But sometimes we need comfort and encouragement. Encouragement should also be on the biblical fellowship agenda. Encouragement is the food of the heart, and every heart is a hungry heart. It can happen intentionally or unintentionally.

A few years ago, my wife gave me an interesting birthday present. She said no to buying me a motorcycle. Instead, she gave me a plant! She said, "You can have this 'Harley-dendra' plant instead." Ha-ha. (Neither one of us really knows what kind of plant it is.)

This might surprise you, but I love that plant, and I've managed to keep it alive for a long time, because I put it in a place where I come into regular contact with it. I keep track of what's going on with the plant. When I see it looking thirsty, I give it a drink. Unfortunately, sometimes I don't notice it needs a drink until it is wilting.

That "Harley-dendra" plant represents a lot of us. Perhaps you can identify. You're wilting, and you need a "drink" of encouragement. The best option is to "drink" regularly and not wait till you're wilting. But it's hard to drink if no one's around to give it to you!

Let me tell you about a specific time in my own life. I didn't know I needed water. I wasn't wilting. A young woman from work gave a testimony about how God had been working in her life. I was overcome as I listened to her story of a father who had abandoned her. She grew up in a broken home, but she described how God had redeemed all of that and used it all for good.

She was twenty-four. At the time, my daughter was twenty-six and was preparing to get married. As I listened, I was so overwhelmed with God's grace to me and to my daughter. I realized that, but by God's grace, I could easily have become just like that other father.

How about you? How close have you come to abandoning everything? Or perhaps you have left everything behind. Have you seen God redeem the situation and teach you about His grace, even in the middle of your rebellion?

In my case, I quit high school. One brother died from an overdose of drugs and alcohol. Another brother is a recovering alcoholic. Another brother has struggled with employment all his life.

I think we all can imagine where I probably would have ended up without God's intervention. Yet God redeemed my situation, and when I heard that young lady's story, I was reminded of His grace and mercy. I took a "drink," and I was encouraged. That's another part of what it means to have biblical fellowship.

How do I know that Jesus is alive? Because I see Him in you. How do I know that Jesus really loves me? Because you really love me. None of us is complete, but together, we are whole. In His wisdom, God has not given any of us everything we need. Instead He chose to give us one another.

Suggestions for Pursuing the Discipline of Fellowship

1. Get into or start a men's small group.

Many men do not naturally pursue relationships. Often men tend to focus more on task and responsibility. Yet God calls us to live in community with other believers. For some of us, that will require an act of the will. We will have to intentionally seek out relationships with other Christian men.

I challenge you to do that. Surround yourself with men who will hold you accountable. Sometimes I will ask a friend, "Do you need a hug or a kick in the pants?" Search out friends who will give you a needed kick in the pants through exhortation, or who will encourage and strengthen you when you need a drink of encouragement. You may find those people at church, or among Christian friends at work, or in a group that gathers to pursue a specific hobby or interest. In my own life, I've discovered them everywhere—but you won't see them till you're looking for them. So incorporate this discipline into your life, and let people fill your gaps, even as you fill theirs.

2. Get into a men's small-group Bible study.

Someone once asked Billy Graham, "If you were a pastor of a large church in a principal city, what would be your plan of action?"

I would have imagined that Mr. Graham would outline a mass evangelistic plan to take the city by storm. Instead, Robert Coleman reported in *The Master Plan of Evangelism* that Graham answered, "I think one of the first things I would do would be to get a small group of eight or ten or twelve men around me that would meet a few hours a week and pay the price! It would cost them something in time and effort. I would share with them everything I have, over a period of years. Then I would actually have twelve ministers among the laymen who in turn could take eight or ten or twelve more and teach them."[1]

Not a bad idea. It's been done before with some success (smile).

3. Get involved with people in your church.

The sheep the wolf goes after is the one that got separated from the flock. Don't separate from your flock. If you're not in church, why not? It's completely biblical to do so, and completely unwise not to do so. Besides, so many rich and rewarding encounters are given and received when we regularly assemble with other Christian believers. Don't try to be a Lone Ranger Christian.

Suggested Spiritual Exercises

- Ask around and see what kind of men's small groups are available in your church. Ask if you can visit one without any obligation, to observe for a few weeks. If you like it, join or start one of your own.

- Ask three men to take *The Three-Week Accountability Challenge.* Think of three other men with whom you think you are compatible. Ask each of them to read the article "How to Have an Accountable Relationship," which may be read or downloaded at www.maninthemirror.org/spiritualdisciplines. Next, commit to meet together for three weeks. Follow or adapt the guide in the article. At the end of three weeks, reevaluate. If any man isn't led to continue, find another to take his place. Order free wallet-sized Accountability Cards (which can be laminated) by phoning Man in the Mirror at 407-472-2100.

Our dearest Father, when we look at the Trinity, we see that You are in relationship: Father, Son, and Holy Spirit. What fellowship You must have with one another. Lord, we pray that You would help us to understand our need for fellowship, and to practice this discipline even when we don't feel like it—especially when we are wilting. Help us drink of the friendship we can offer one another. We ask this in the power and the name of Jesus. Amen.

A Review of the Big Ideas

ೢ Like redwoods, we will find it's easier to stand strong when we stand together.

ೢ I know God is real because I can see Him in you.

ೢ We all have different parts to play in this body. God designed us that way on purpose, so that we need one another to survive as a body.

ೢ In His wisdom God has not given any of us everything we need to follow Him successfully. Instead He chose to give us one another.

ೢ How do I know that Jesus is alive? Because I see Him in you. How do I know that Jesus really loves me? Because you really love me.

ೢ Search out friends who will give you a needed kick in the pants through exhortation, or who will encourage and strengthen you when you need a drink of encouragement.

Discussion Questions

1. How has someone spurred you on or encouraged you recently—maybe a family member or someone in your small group? How did it make you feel?

2. Hebrews 10:24–25 makes fellowship mandatory. Do you agree or disagree? Explain your answer.

3. What barriers keep men from enjoying genuine fellowship with one another?

4. Do you need to "give" or "get" more genuine Christian fellowship? Explain your answer. What will you do about it?

Additional Resources

Brothers! Calling Men into Vital Relationships by Geoff Gorsuch with Dan Schaffer

7

A MAN AND COUNSEL

PREVIEW

In this chapter we will:

- **Discover why men need to seek and receive counsel from one another.**
- **Explore eight principles to guide the process of seeking counsel.**

Early in the 2001 NASCAR season, Steve Park had everything going for him. He was driving for Dale Earnhardt, Inc. (DEI) and a big corporate sponsor, Penzoil. He even drove the big number "1" car.

Park was racing in the Nextel Cup Series—the top league in stock cars, the "brass ring." Yet, like a lot of other guys, Park wanted to drive in other leagues as well. He admitted that he was begging DEI to let him drive a Busch car, part of a less prestigious stock car league than Nextel. But his employers along with representatives from Penzoil said, "No. We don't want you risking your career on a Busch race."

Finally, because he kept insisting, they relented and let him run. Park said, "Then their worst fear was realized. Exactly what they told me over and over they were afraid would happen, did happen."

In September of 2001 Park's career took a significant downward turn when he crashed at the "Lady in Black," the Darlington Speedway in South Carolina. Park was driving under a caution flag, readying for a restart, when he was involved in an accident. His car came to rest against the inside wall, and he stayed pinned in the vehicle for twenty minutes, waiting to be extricated from the wreckage. Rescue workers finally had to cut away the car roof to get him out.

Park suffered a concussion, and he had to sit out the rest of the 2001 season and the beginning of the 2002 season. In 2001 he had been a title contender. In 2002 he was ranked thirty-eighth. He finished out the 2003 racing season and then was released, no longer needed.

Steve Park's story is our story. We may choose a course of action without taking counsel, without considering God's plans and desires. We're not really looking for His will, because we've already decided what we want to do. Like Park pleading with his owners and sponsor, we beg and beg— of people and sometimes God—to get what we want. Even when wise and experienced people give good counsel to go in a different direction, we choose to go our own way. And the price of going our own way is getting our own way. Perhaps the secret of contentment is not getting what we want, but wanting what we get.

The Discipline of Seeking and Accepting Wise Counsel

Counsel on Moral Decisions

I'm fairly certain that among my readers, a percentage of you are currently deciding whether to divorce your wives. How do I know this? Because I've been involved in Bible studies for men for three decades, and every year with each group attending my Bible study, several men divorce their wives. It can happen. If you fall into that category considering divorce, let me ask you: Do you want counsel about that?

Further, I can guarantee that some of my readers are involved in sexual affairs with women other than their wives. Perhaps you're trying to decide if you should break it off. Do you really want counsel about that?

Those are moral decisions, and your choices will affect you for the rest of your life. They probably will affect other people as well, though we usually don't like to consider that. If we are wise, we will seek God's will. And sometimes the best way to discover that is by asking advice from men who know God well.

Proverbs 15:22 says, "Plans fail for lack of counsel, but with many advisers they succeed." Now, remember, a proverb is defined as being generally true, but there can be some exceptions. So in general, plans tend to fail without counsel, or seeking advice. And generally, with adequate counseling, they succeed.

Bible Truths about Counsel

Verses throughout the book of Proverbs underscore this truth. As you read the following verses, consider taking a moment to write the main theme of each in the space provided.

- "The way of a fool seems right to him, but a wise man listens to advice" (Proverbs 12:15).

  _____

- "A mocker resents correction; he will not consult the wise" (Proverbs 15:12).

  _____

- "Make plans by seeking advice; if you wage war, obtain guidance" (Proverbs 20:18).

  _____

- "For waging war you need guidance, and for victory many advisers" (Proverbs 24:6).

  _____

- "He who trusts in himself is a fool, but he who walks in wisdom is kept safe" (Proverbs 28:26).

  _____

Living Out a Commitment to Seeking Counsel

If we are going to seek counsel, we must be humble enough to admit we don't have all the answers. This requires discipline and intention, because it's not something that comes naturally.

When I look at the terrible decisions I've made, I see a correlation between the level of my stupidity and the degree to which I have not sought advice from other people. We all have a big problem when it comes to decision making. Generally, we see the situation from only one viewpoint —and often we see only what we want to see.

One day I ate lunch with a man who had asked me for advice two years earlier. He said, "Pat, I am thinking about putting a mortgage on my house and taking my savings and putting it into a franchise business. What do you think?"

I replied, "You really don't want to hear what I have to say. Why go through the ruse of asking? You've already decided what you want to do, and you're going to do it, regardless of what I say."

I was right. He did it, and after another two years we had lunch again. He'd lost his life's savings and his house. You can say he was crazy to risk his home on a start-up business—but his problem affects all of us when it comes to decision making. The problem is self-deceit.

Demosthenes, the greatest orator of his time, said, "Nothing is easier than self-deceit, for what each man wishes, that he also believes to be true." I've never met anyone who is not subject to self-deceit. And the greatest self-deceit of all is that we're not susceptible.

Let's take a look at Hebrews 3:13, which says, "But encourage one another . . ." In the previous chapter we discussed fellowship, and I noted that in His wisdom, God does not give any person everything he needs. Instead He gives us the gift of one another. So this is part of the "one another." Counsel flows from fellowship.

Let's go back to that verse. "But encourage one another daily, as long as it is called Today, so that none of you may be hardened by sin's deceitfulness." Therein lies the problem. A made-up mind is almost impossible to change. We don't ask for counsel because we don't really want it. We don't take counsel because we don't like what we hear.

Most people do not want counsel—they want permission. They've already decided what they want to do, and now they want evidence and support for the decisions they've already made. We saw that with NASCAR's Steve Park, but we see it in ourselves as well. To live out this discipline, we must settle the heart issues first. Ask yourself, "Do I really want to make a wise decision, or do I just want to have my own way?"

Suggestions for Pursuing Wise Counsel

Scripture tells us to seek advice from many people, but it also gives instances of biblical figures who sought advice from the wrong people, with disastrous results. For example, in 2 Chronicles 10, Rehoboam rejected the wise advice of his father Solomon's counselors in favor of the foolish advice of the young men he had grown up with.

So let's look at how we should seek counsel, keeping in mind that godly counsel exposes self-deceit. Theologians talk about a concept called *the noetic influence of sin*. This refers to the influence of sin on the mind *(nous)*. Theologians tell us that, when Adam and Eve sinned, it affected not just the body and the emotions, but also the mind. The apostle Paul noted this when he wrote, "Now I know in part; then I shall know fully, even as I am fully known" (1 Corinthians 13:12). Our minds are limited and fallible. They make mistakes, and that's why we need counsel.

Let's focus on a decision you're facing right now. You don't know whether to go left or right. You don't know whether you should stop or go backwards. I want to give eight practical suggestions to help you seek godly counsel.

1. Understand that decisions fall into two categories.

Every decision you make will be either a moral or priority decision. Moral choices are choices between right and wrong. When a man asks any of the following questions, he is about to make a moral decision:

"Is it really that bad to fib a little when I calculate my taxes?"

"Can I enter into a relationship with someone other than my wife without getting caught?"

"Who will get hurt if I fudge on my résumé?"

Priority choices are decisions between right and right. Here are two examples:

"Should I invest in this stock, or in that stock?"

"Which car should I buy?"

If you need counsel on a moral issue, go to someone with moral authority and knowledge. Seek counsel from people who know the Scriptures. That doesn't necessarily apply if you're making a priority decision. If you want to buy a good used car, you won't seek advice from a pastor or Bible study leader—unless, of course, they are really smart about cars.

2. Ask yourself, "Am I decided or undecided?"

If you've already decided what you want to do, you'll seek counsel differently than if you really haven't made up your mind. You might be tentative about your decision, so you seek confirmation. Or you might really not know how to proceed. If you have already decided, I'd suggest you still should open yourself up to counsel, and be willing to listen.

3. Distinguish between human ingenuity and God's wisdom.

God's wisdom is found in the Scriptures, and it is administered through the Holy Spirit. Many men—like lawyers, counselors, and pastors—give all kinds of wisdom. But you must decide whether you're getting human ingenuity or godly wisdom.

I am an idea person. I make ideas like popcorn machines make popcorn. The problem is, most of these ideas are terrible. Over the years, I've realized that most of my ideas are born out of human ingenuity, not godly wisdom.

So I don't rush into the office on Tuesdays for team meetings and say, "We need to do this or we need to do that." I say, "Here are the ideas I've been thinking about this week. Which ones do you think might be worth pursuing?" We talk about it; we counsel. I don't say, "We're going to do this," because I've learned better.

4. Choose your counselor based on your need for reason or passion.

Figure out whether you need to hear from the voice of reason or the voice of passion. If you are facing a moral decision, and you already know the right thing to do, you don't need the voice of reason. You need the voice of passion. You need someone to encourage and inspire and motivate you to do the right thing. You need someone to say, "You can do this. You can make it happen."

If you're muddled and confused, and don't know which way to go, you need the voice of reason. Analyze your situation, so you know what kind of person to choose as your adviser.

5. Beware of the counselor with the quick answer.

Suppose you've been wrestling with an excruciating problem for many months. You go to someone seeking advice. You get out about three or four sentences. You unburden your heart a bit. And the counselor jumps in and says, "Let me tell you what to do."

Too many people will give *counselor*-oriented counsel (versus *counselee*-oriented counsel). Generally, they're not in your situation, and they don't take enough time to understand the "guts" of your problem. They are quick to tell you what *they* would do, but they don't get to know enough about your issue to help you understand what *you* ought to do. Find someone who's willing to listen – someone who asks questions and tries to draw you out instead of telling you immediately what you should do.

6. Remember that some people have agendas.

Employees have agendas. Salesmen have agendas. When you seek advice from someone, it's probably good to know if that person has a heart for you, or if he is seeking a particular outcome. For instance, it's stupid to expect objective advice from somebody who will gain financially if you say yes and lose financially if you say no. That doesn't necessarily mean their advice is bad. In fact, it probably will be good. So go ahead and talk to that person. Get all the available information. But then go to someone who is for you and get additional counsel.

7. Don't explode, don't pout, and don't put down.

What is the best way to get bad advice? Repeatedly chase away good advice. In the Old Testament, King Ahab's counselors gave horrible advice, because every time an advisor said something the king didn't like, he'd slash off his head or put the counselor in jail. Don't chafe at advice—even if you didn't seek it. Recently a long-time ministry supporter took a strong exception to something I had said and gave me some unsolicited advice. Instead of blowing him off, I asked a couple of our key executives, "What can we learn from him? What is the spiritual way to respond?"

If you want honest, thoughtful advice, welcome any input, even the negative. Express gratitude—not judgment or frustration—with all advice you receive.

8. Peace is the umpire.

You've sought counsel, and it feels emotionally right. It makes sense. It reasons well. You feel peace. I believe that, as godly wisdom exposes itself, you'll know your answer when you come to that place of peace.

Whatever decision you are facing, I encourage you to seek wise counsel. Some readers are making priority decisions. Others are making moral decisions. I encourage you to find some trustworthy Christian brothers. Be honest with one another; open up. Seek counsel. Remember Proverbs 15:22: "Plans fail for lack of counsel, but with many advisers they succeed." Also, remember to review this chapter in the future when you are up against a tough one.

Heavenly Father, thank You for the gift of one another. We all are subject to self-deceit, so I ask You to call to our minds this gift You have given for seeking counsel. Help us recognize it as the solution to our problem of self-deceit. None of us wants to fail. By seeking counsel we enhance our probabilities of hearing Your voice. Help us see the value of seeking counsel, so we will also do it. We ask this in the name of Jesus. Amen.

A Review of the Big Ideas

❧ We're not really looking for His will, because we've already decided what we want to do.

❧ Most people do not want counsel—they want permission.

❧ The price of going our own way is getting our own way.

❧ Before we seek counsel, we must be humble enough to admit we don't have all the answers.

❧ All decisions fall into two categories: moral and priority.

❧ Distinguish between human ingenuity and God's wisdom.

❧ Beware of the counselor who is too quick with an answer.

❧ Peace is the umpire.

Discussion Questions

1. Describe either:

• a plan that failed for lack of counsel, or

• a plan that succeeded because of wise counsel.

2. What are the problems that are solved by seeking counsel according to Proverbs 15:22; 20:18; 20:5; and Hebrews 13:10?

3. This chapter lists eight suggestions for filtering and sifting the counsel you receive. Which suggestion did you most need to hear, and why?

• Moral or priority choices

• Decided or undecided

- Human ingenuity or God's wisdom

- Voice of passion or voice of reason

- Focused on counselor vs. focused on counselee

- Counselor who's for you or for a particular outcome

- Don't explode, pout, or put down

- Peace is the umpire

4. What one thing do you need counsel about right now? Who can best provide advice?

8

A MAN AND FASTING

PREVIEW

In this chapter we'll:

- **Show why fasting remains an important discipline.**

- **Learn its purpose and its benefits**

- **Give specific instructions for those who want to pursue fasting as an expression of their love for God.**

In my commute to the office, I pass three grocery stores, at least eleven fast-food restaurants, two pizza places, two Chinese takeouts, an ice cream parlor, and two convenience stores advertising specific snack items on roadside signs. We live in a world built around convenience and instant gratification, especially when it comes to food. There's not much of an audience for the message of self-denial. In essence, we aren't very good at saying no to ourselves.

That's why fasting—giving up food for a specific period of time—is a discipline. It doesn't come naturally. Yet fasting is a biblical discipline. Fasting is probably not for the new Christian. You certainly would never announce at your new members class, "To help you get acquainted with our church, we're asking you to join a two-year Bible study that will examine Christianity in the original Greek, and we're going to kick it off with a forty-day fast!"

As we have noted with other disciplines, fasting does not "buy" more love or attention from God. It does not earn His favor. It does not improve a person's place in some Christian pecking order. Fasting is simply a tool to help us remove distractions and focus more clearly on relating to God and pursuing His will. When you slow down your physiological life, there can be an expansion on the spiritual side of your life. In fact, the acuity, the sharpness, of our mental faculties goes up when the blood is not focusing on the digestive process.

For some of you, this discipline is exactly what you've been looking for. You've been longing for a deeper relationship with Jesus. You've been wondering, *How can I humble myself before such a Holy God? How can I find wisdom for these incredible, difficult decisions I have to make? How can I find peace for the impossible situation I find myself in?* You've been reading the Bible over and over and praying over and over, and there is still something missing.

For others, you really have never thought much about this idea of fasting, and yet, by the end of this chapter, fasting is going to look very attractive to you.

Fasting through the Years

As contemporary Christians, we must understand that, while fasting may run counter to our culture, it does not run counter to Scripture. Throughout the Bible narrative men fasted, including Moses, David, Nehemiah, Ezra, Daniel, Jeremiah, Isaiah, and even Jesus (who began His ministry with a forty-day fast). We know from Scripture and also from extrabiblical literature that fasting was common during the era when Jesus lived on earth.

The book of Acts reveals that fasting was a regular practice in the early church (for example, Acts 10:30 KJV; 13:2–3; 14:23). Scripture also reveals that Paul fasted (2 Corinthians 11:27). An overview of Christian history reveals that Martin Luther, John Calvin, John Knox, John Wesley, Jonathan Edwards, Charles Finney, and other great leaders believed in the value of fasting and practiced it in their own lives.

So if we have so many biblical and historical references to this discipline, why do so few contemporary people pursue this discipline? Mainly, the church in the Middle Ages supported a severely ascetic and monastic lifestyle. The modern move away from fasting was, in part, a reaction to that.

Affluence also seems to diminish the attraction to disciplines of self-denial. But times of difficulty tend to restore our focus. We saw that after the terrorist attacks on September 11, 2001. All across America, people were suddenly focused on spiritual issues.

We've seen fasting at other times as well. Take, for instance, the Civil War. A full 364,000 Americans died as a result of that war. That was roughly one out of every hundred Americans! Both presidents—Abraham Lincoln and Jefferson Davis—declared days of fasting and prayer. By 1865 the war was over, and slavery, one of history's most evil institutions, was dismantled in the United States. No doubt, the national fasting and prayer profoundly impacted the abolition of slavery.

Then fasting fell into disfavor again. Bill Bright and others have noted that, between the years 1861 and 1954, not one single book was written on the subject of fasting. Then on July 5, 1994, Bill Bright, founder of Campus Crusade for Christ, felt led by God to go on a forty-day fast.

I was heavily involved with him at that time as a member of Campus Crusade's board of directors, so I was with him several times during those forty days. When he ended the fast, I went to the meeting where he challenged Christians around the world to pursue fasting. An estimated two million people around the world responded, Dr. Bright later reported.

There Is a Time to Fast

As we've noted, fasting was relatively prevalent in the time in which Jesus lived on earth—and Jesus Himself fasted before He began His ministry (Matthew 4:1–3). But often Jesus chose not to fast. So the religious leaders questioned His spirituality. At one point they commented to Him, "John's disciples often fast and pray and so do the disciples of the Pharisees" (Luke 5:33). So fasting was prevalent in Jesus' day, but His disciples continued eating and drinking.

Jesus answered their implied question, "Why won't You fast, Jesus?" in the next verses, saying, "Can you make the guests for the bridegroom fast while He is with them?" He added, "The time will come when the bridegroom will be taken away from them; in those days they will fast." Allow me to paraphrase. In essence, Jesus said, "There's a time when fasting is appropriate, and a time when it is not." So now is the time to fast.

The Purposes and Benefits of Fasting

Fasting involves giving up something you normally do, for the purpose of focusing more time and attention on God. Fasting is also an excellent way to express sorrow to God, to be penitent to the Lord. Sometimes men do things that are so overwhelming and despicable to them, they just can't accept forgiveness and let them go. Fasting enables men to express the depth of their remorse, because it expresses humility. During fasting, they often are reminded of a holy, transcendent God who seeks their obedience and yet shows compassion. Fasting also helps the participant to focus on how to avoid repeating a negative behavior pattern. In addition, if you are struggling with pride or anger, fasting is a tangible expression of humility before God.

The most common type of fasting involves giving up food. Other fasts might include water, one meal, certain types of food, giving up going out to eat, or even non-food items, such as movies or television. In my own experience, when I de-emphasize satisfying my physical appetites, I expand spiritually.

Fasting has many benefits:

1. *Fasting adds strength to the participant's prayer life.* The gospels of Matthew and Mark both record an instance where a father brought his demon-possessed boy for ministry. The disciples were not able to help, but Jesus commanded the deaf and mute spirit to leave, and the boy was restored. The disciples asked why they were not successful, and Jesus told them, "This kind only leaves because of prayer and fasting" (Matthew 17:21; Mark 9:29; both KJV). Fasting increases the power of prayer.

2. *Fasting helps the participant to hear God's voice and receive His direction.* Sometimes we must make tough decisions. For instance, a manager may face an agonizing requirement to let some people go at work because business is not so good. Or a guy in his forties may be diagnosed with a disease that has more than one treatment option. Or a young father may have difficulty figuring out how to discipline one of his children. In each case, the man's choice is rarely black and white, and no matter how he chooses, he sees potential for both positive and negative results. Sometimes you just don't have enough wisdom. Fasting is an excellent way to seek God's direction.

3. *Fasting releases the participant from the confusion of competing voices.* Your personality and temperament will affect the kinds of things that distract you from relationship with God. For me, it's work. I'm a recovering workaholic. I love production. I love creativity. I love to work. If I'm not careful on any given day, I can literally work myself into a stupor. I've discovered fasting as a way to slow down my "RPMs," protecting my focus on Jesus Christ.

4. *Fasting allows the participant to express love to God in a tangible way.* Cultural Christianity doesn't require much sacrifice. We are a blessed people. Even the poorest among us are wealthier than the majority of people in a developing country. So we face a serious question— if we never sacrifice anything for Jesus, how can we truly be sure that we love Him? Fasting is a tangible demonstration of your commitment to Christ. Pursuing fasting as a discipline expresses that your love for Him is greater than your love for physical comfort. It helps you bring your faith-walk into alignment with Scripture, for as Jesus reminded Satan, "Man does not live on bread alone" (see Luke 4:4; Deuteronomy 8:3).

My History with Fasting

A friend, Ted Bywater, first encouraged me to get involved with fasting back in the 1980s. Since then, fasting has been a regular part of my life.
It was a Monday afternoon, two o'clock. I had just returned from

lunch, and now fatigue swept over me. I had been calling on the Lord for months and months. My emotions were raw from the series of ups and downs, and I felt I could not bear another minute of these problems.

Sitting at my desk and talking on the phone with Ted, I decided I would fast as an act of faith. I trusted God to honor this and reveal His will, His purpose, and His plan. I didn't actually delineate how I would know when the fast should end, and I couldn't define what I was seeking from the Lord. I only knew I could not go on at status quo. I decided to fast until God answered, or until I died!

I called my wife, Patsy, and told her my decision. Patsy has always been very careful to listen for God's voice. That afternoon, she seemed to be filled with a reverent respect for what I was announcing, confirming in my mind that the idea was from God.

I fasted for perhaps four days. Nothing really changed except my heart. That was 1981. The circumstances of the previous months had made me feel like a bird, locked in a cage with lead weights on its feet. After the fast, I felt as if He had removed the weights and opened the door. I was flying again. But my circumstances had not changed.

Fasting for an Ailing Friend . . . and with Many Leaders

That put me on the road to experiment with fasting. Then in 1985, a friend developed incurable hepatitis B. In 1989, he was going downhill for a lot of reasons, so I committed to fast one day a week for him until he was healed. I would skip dinner at night, then breakfast and lunch the following day, resuming meals with dinner the following night. I went about my normal business, though I would get fatigued in the afternoons and sometimes would lie down for a ten- or twenty-minute nap. I did that for forty weeks.

A lot of other people were praying for my friend too, so I want to be careful not to suggest a one-to-one correlation here. Nevertheless, my friend was completely healed.

In December of 1994, Bill Bright initiated a special day of fasting and called a meeting of leaders in Orlando, I joined the six hundred who were fasting and decided to try the forty-day fast he challenged us to attempt. I bought a juicer and started the fast. After a week, my appetite was completely gone. However, after about the tenth day, I started to become irritable. I became more and more irritable every day. On the fourteenth day, I had to pull the plug on it. I figured, "I am not made to do a forty-day fast."

Later that year, we needed some direction at our ministry, Man in the Mirror, so I called for a day of prayer and fasting. There were five of us at the time, and I was surprised to learn the other four had never fasted. That was in 1995. Today this ministry touches millions of men, and we always point right back to that meeting. Fasting released spiritual power, and the results are still being seen more than a decade later.

From 1995 to 2005 I fasted one day a week—a twenty-four-hour fast from dinner to dinner, skipping breakfast and lunch. I could pretty much handle my normal schedule, because it was not an extended period.

I do not currently fast. In late 2004 I started racing sports cars for recreation. By early 2005, I realized I needed to increase my endurance for racing, so began a rigorous one-hour per day workout schedule. Right now fasting doesn't fit into my physically demanding schedule, so I have completely stopped. Certainly I feel no less connected to God. In the future I will no doubt again fast, perhaps regularly—I don't know. For now, I have other ways to express my devotion to God. And I certainly never thought fasting made me "better," so not fasting sure doesn't make me any "worse."

Suggestions for Pursuing the Discipline of Fasting

Your Attitude

Scripture doesn't just tell us that fasting is a worthwhile discipline to pursue. It also gives some specific instruction about the attitude that should accompany the discipline.

In Matthew 6:16–17, Jesus said, "When you fast, do not look somber as the hypocrites do, for they disfigure their faces to show men they are fasting. I tell you the truth, they have received their reward in full."

Jesus condemns the attitude that causes us to seek praise from people by letting them know about the fasting. In the subsequent verses, He basically tells His followers, "Get dressed, go to work, continue your normal lifestyle, shave your face, and look normal." That way, Jesus says, "it will not be obvious to men that you are fasting but only to your Father, who is unseen. And your Father, who sees what is done in secret, will reward you."

Does this mean that if anybody ever finds out that you're fasting, you've defeated your purpose? No, that's a little legalistic. This passage simply says, "Don't make it obvious to people that you're fasting."

That doesn't mean I don't tell anyone. For example, when I'm fasting, my wife needs to know, because she would be very irritated if she made a meal and I said, "I'm sorry, I can't eat that."

She'd ask, "Why not?"

"Oh," I'd reply. "I can't tell you—it's a secret."

I'm sure you're getting the picture here. Trust me—you don't have to be legalistic about this.

Your Preparation before the Fast

If you want to do a three- or four-day fast, you probably need to prepare. For example, stop taking caffeine—for most of us, that's coffee—and get ready for the caffeine headache. Don't try to maintain your regular exercise regimen as you forego all those calories. If you intend to fast for longer than a day, you should probably back off heavy exercise and maybe do a little walking instead.

When you are fasting, reserve the time you normally would be consuming food, and use it instead to read the Bible and pray. I don't see any magic formula here. I can't tell you how long to pray, but if you've never tried this before, you might want to skip one meal and see what happens. Depending on your schedule, choose a weekday or a weekend day. You might want to just skip breakfast and devote the morning to prayer.

Physical Aspects of Fasting

Some people take in nothing but water. Others drink juice as well, to keep their energy levels constant with the intake of sugar. I don't think most men can reasonably expect to maintain a normal schedule without some glucose. I take a half glass of orange juice and mix it with half a glass of water. Apple juice and watermelon juice are also good for this.

I also encourage you to consider if you have medical issues affected by a lack of food. For instance, if you have diabetes or high blood pressure, please check with your doctor before you try this. If you get tired during the day, take a nap. Maybe that's the body saying you need to rest.

Fasting does have some "side effects." You may experience acute hunger pangs. You might get a stomachache or headache. When you fast, the body cleanses itself. Sometimes that causes bad breath, so keep some mints so you don't offend people at work.

And when you start eating again, don't rush down to the local fast food joint to order a burger and fries. Instead, eat a banana or something that doesn't have a lot of fatty content.

A Sacrifice

And remember—the point of all this isn't to earn a pat on the back from God. The point is to tangibly demonstrate our love for Him and our desire to lead a more holy life. Again, if we never sacrifice anything for Jesus, how is He going to know that we love Him? How are we going to know that we love Him? Fasting is a wonderful discipline to make such a sacrifice.

Fasting gives us an opportunity to satisfy our spiritual appetite by sacrificing our physical appetite. It recognizes the value of Jesus' promise: "Blessed are they who hunger and thirst for righteousness, for they will be filled" (see Matthew 5:6).

Heavenly Father, thank You for the discipline of fasting. Because it's in Your Scripture, while it may fall into disuse, it's never lost. I know, Lord, that at least half of the men I meet are hurting. They are facing circumstances beyond their wisdom. They're beyond their emotional strength. They're fatigued. They don't see a way out. They face all kinds of problems, and I believe they can be helped through the discipline of fasting. As they commit to that, I'm asking You to reveal Yourself in a deeper, more powerful way. I ask this in the name of Your Son, Jesus. Amen.

A Review of the Big Ideas

❧ Fasting gives us an opportunity to satisfy our spiritual appetite by sacrificing our physical appetite.

❧ Throughout the Bible men fasted, including Moses, David, Daniel, Jeremiah, Isaiah, and even Jesus (who began His ministry with a forty-day fast).

❧ Fasting involves giving up something you normally do, for the purpose of focusing more time and attention on God.

❧ Fasting allows the participant to express sorrow and penitence.

❧ Fasting strengthens the participant's prayer life.

❧ Fasting allows the participant to express love to God in a tangible way.

❧ If we never sacrifice anything for Jesus, how can we truly be sure that we love Him?

Discussion Questions

1. What is the purpose of fasting?

2. Fasting is an integral part of the Bible. Many biblical characters fasted, including Ezra, Nehemiah, Esther, Samuel, David, Isaiah, Jeremiah, Daniel, Zechariah, Jesus, John (the Baptist), and Paul. Jesus began His ministry with a forty-day fast. We've mentioned several portions of Scripture in this chapter. What conclusions can you draw about fasting from these biblical texts from the New Testament?

Luke 5:33–35

2 Corinthians 11:27

Matthew 6:16–17

3. Have you ever fasted and, if so, when, why, and what happened? Do you have any inclination to try fasting now and, if so, what are your initial thoughts about when, why, and how?

4. In what area do you struggle to gain victory? Or in what area do you need wisdom? Have you tried fasting about it? If not, would you like to?

9

A MAN AND SPIRITUAL WARFARE

PREVIEW

In this chapter, we will see how the daily discipline of spiritual warfare can help us determine and follow God's will. We'll:

- **Face the temptation to accept two lies:**

  1) the public lie that we have defeated the flesh;
  2) the private lie that we cannot conquer the flesh.

- **See how ignoring our natural desires and enlisting the help of a trustworthy community can help us win the battle between flesh and spirit.**

My friend David Delk, president of Man in the Mirror, tells the story about an orange tree in his backyard. Suppose David grew tired of oranges, deciding he wanted apples instead. What if he went to the grocery store and bought a big bag of beautiful, red-cheeked apples and a roll of duct tape. Then suppose he took all the oranges off the tree and taped apples where the oranges had been.

"Would that change the tree?" David asks. "Of course not! Next year the tree would sprout orange blossoms, which would give way to oranges —not apples."

The reason, as David reminds me and others, is you can't change the fruit if you don't change the root. The only way to get rid of the oranges is to dig the tree up by its roots and start over again by planting a different kind of tree.

What Is Spiritual Warfare?

Changing your outward behavior isn't the goal of any spiritual discipline. That would be like putting fresh paint over rusty metal. Willpower alone is no good until it flows from belief, expressed as true surrender to Christ's lordship. So the goal of each spiritual discipline is to trust Christ more. Learning to surrender to Jesus as Lord is what the discipline of spiritual warfare is all about.

If you've already read eight chapters of this book, I'm comfortable assuming that you want to be "good," that is, righteous. Yet I also think it is fair to say that every man has some persistent temptations that get in the way of achieving his goal of righteousness. Unmanaged, these temptations boil over into sin. Different men struggle with different issues. For some it may be lust and pornography. For others it may be greed and always wanting more money. For still others it may be anger, even rage. For some it may be fear and cowardice. The list of specific temptations could go on forever, but the bottom line is, we all struggle with something—some of us with a combination of things.

Even the apostle Paul was not immune to this human frailty. He wrote, "I do not understand what I do. For what I want to do I do not do, but what I hate to do . . . For I have the desire to do what is good, but I cannot carry it out . . . When I want to do good, evil is right there with me" (Romans 7:15, 18, 21). He described the battle between God's law and the "law of sin." He said his natural desires "wage war" against his supernatural desires, and he saw himself as a "prisoner" in need of God's rescue, through the ministry of Jesus Christ (Romans 7:22–25).

Why Is Spiritual Warfare Important?

As the previous passage explains, our lives are a battleground between natural and supernatural—between flesh and spirit. When we become Christians, we are forgiven, made new, given eternal life. Second Corinthians 5:17 tells us we are a "new creation." John 3:5–8 says we are "born of the Spirit."

All of that is true, but the everyday reality is that we live out that newness in a strange tension between the natural and the supernatural. When we become Christians, we don't become purely spiritual beings. We still live in human bodies, with human motivations and desires.

Because of that, Paul encourages Christians to "live by the Spirit, and you will not gratify the desires of the sinful nature." He adds that the old sinful nature loves to do evil, which is just the opposite of what the Holy Spirit desires (Galatians 5:16–17).

These two forces—the sinful nature and the Holy Spirit—constantly war against each other, so that our choices are never free from this conflict. That is the most basic definition of spiritual warfare. This conflict is the core of the Christian struggle, reflected in our moment-by-moment choices to live by our agendas or by God's. If we are wise, we will enter into this battle as disciplined soldiers, engaging in spiritual warfare as a daily habit.

Living Out a Commitment to Spiritual Warfare

Paul told first-century Christians they were "called to be free." But he warned, "Do not use your freedom to indulge the sinful nature" (Galatians 5:13). Through Christ, we gain access to the armor and the weaponry that will free us from bondage to temptation and sin. But usually that freedom doesn't come automatically. It requires our participation.

It's easy to know if we are winning or losing the war. "The acts of the sinful nature are obvious," Paul explained, listing "sexual immorality, impurity and debauchery; idolatry and witchcraft; hatred, discord, jealousy, fits of rage, selfish ambition, dissensions, factions and envy; drunkenness, orgies and the like" (Galatians 5:19–21). People who live like that apart from trust in Christ are losing the battle.

On the other hand, people who are winning exhibit the "fruit of the Spirit," which Paul describes as "love, joy, peace, patience, kindness, goodness, faithfulness, gentleness and self-control." People who demonstrate these qualities are "in step with the Spirit" (Galatians 5:22–25). They are winning the spiritual battle, and they enjoy the favor and peace of our great God.

Throughout this passage, Paul challenges us to cooperate with God in this process. Most of us realize our participation is required, but in our efforts to achieve superiority over ourselves, we face two potential errors. If we accept either of these lies, we will miss the joy and freedom of long-term obedience to God.

1. *We publicly pretend we have conquered the flesh.* No one can win this war in his own strength. We win only through the Holy Spirit. Don't ever pretend that you aren't a sinful man. It is very dangerous to pretend that you have conquered that which you have not. Even if you are victorious most of the time, you face a new struggle with every new situation and every new decision. You win each battle only by God's supernatural power to free you from your limitations.

2. *We privately deny the possibility of conquering the flesh.* We all face a temptation to look at Scripture with disbelieving eyes. We see our unique experiences as somehow different from those recorded in our Bibles. We think, "I like what it says here, but it must be describing something others can overcome by the Spirit, not me." That response denies scriptural truth. Our text says if you "live by the Spirit, you will not gratify the desires of the sinful nature" (Galatians 5:16). No exceptions are noted.

If you don't pull weeds on a regular basis, you will soon have nothing but weeds. So practice the discipline of spiritual warfare on a regular basis.

Suggestions for Pursuing the Discipline of Spiritual Warfare

In the movie *A Beautiful Mind*, Russell Crowe plays John Nash, a brilliant mathematician who happens to be schizophrenic. In one scene, someone asks Professor Nash if his delusions are gone. "Maybe they never will be," he responds, "but I've gotten used to ignoring them. I think that as a result they have given up on me."

This is a good analogy for how we win a spiritual battle. Temptations may continue repeatedly, but we can conquer them. Here are some suggestions.

1. Subdue your temptations.

Don't feed your temptations. For instance, if you're an alcoholic, don't schedule your business meetings in a bar or go out to lunch with guys who drink martinis. If you struggle with lust and pornography, don't buy a swimsuit calendar. If you lose your temper when you become overstressed, know your warning signs and don't be so driven.

Starve your temptations. Shrink your appetites. We can make tremendous progress if we can just put ourselves out of sin's line of fire.

2. Establish yourself in a community.

In that same movie, Professor Nash asks his nemesis, now a department head at Princeton University, to find a place for him in that institution. He believes that participating in a community might help him. "A certain level of attachment to familiar places and people might help me to elbow out these delusions that I have," he says.

This also is helpful in spiritual warfare. Many centuries ago, Solomon wisely noted, "Two are better than one . . . though one may be overpowered, two can defend themselves. A cord of three strands is not quickly broken" (Ecclesiastes 4:9, 12). It's true in physical battle—there is strength in numbers. But it's true in a spiritual battle as well. When you surround yourself with people who support you, and who share your commitment to living a godly life, you will find help in your struggle.

I am quite confident from experience that at least half of the men reading this book are struggling with something that is absolutely consuming them. They lack power. Most could see victory if they would engage with a trustworthy community.

Find a group of men who will share your struggles and invite them to pray for you. Make yourself vulnerable and open up. Let them restore to you the reality that Scripture is true, and that by living by the Spirit, you can develop habits that oppose the gratification of the sinful nature. This is the central idea in the discipline of spiritual warfare.

3. Put on the full armor of God.

Look at Ephesians 6:13–18:

Put on the full armor of God, so that when the day of evil comes, you may be able to stand your ground, and after you have done everything, to stand. Stand firm then, with the belt of *truth* buckled around your waist, with the breastplate of *righteousness* in place, and with your feet fitted with the readiness that comes from *the gospel* of peace. In addition to all this, take up the shield of *faith*, with which you can extinguish all the flaming arrows of the evil one. Take the helmet of *salvation* and the sword of the Spirit, which is *the word of God*. And *pray* in the Spirit on all occasions with all kinds of prayers and requests. With this in mind, be alert and always keep on praying for all the saints.
(emphasis added)

This passage is the central plan for how to exercise the discipline of spiritual warfare.

No soldier would go to battle in street clothes. Instead, he wants some body armor, and something that shoots back! Our body armor is the "truth" we find in God's Word, righteous living, the gospel, our faith, and our salvation. Our weapon is the sword of the Spirit—the Bible and prayer.

Father, I believe every reader longs to do the right things. We long to please You. And yet we stumble in so many different ways. Help us strip away our masks, so we don't pretend we are conquering when we are not. Lord, in this struggle, let us not deny the efficacy of Your holy Word. I pray that You would help each of us to gain victory over the flesh, over our sinful nature, through the Holy Spirit. I pray that You would use our communities to help in this endeavor. Lord, may each reader see genuine progress in his life, and may he not be discouraged in the meantime. We pray this in the name of Jesus. Amen.

A Review of the Big Ideas

⚜ Every man has some struggle that gets in the way of achieving the goal of righteousness.

⚜ Two forces—the sinful nature and the Holy Spirit—constantly war against each other, so that our choices are never free from this conflict.

⚜ Paul encourages believers to "live by the Spirit, and you will not gratify the desires of the sinful nature."

⚜ Don't ever pretend that you aren't a sinful man. It is very dangerous to pretend that you have conquered that which you have not.

⚜ Subdue your temptations.

⚜ Establish yourself in a community.

⚜ Put on the full armor of God.

Discussion Questions

1. In the movie *A Beautiful Mind*, schizophrenic John Nash, when questioned if his delusional characters were gone, said, "No, they're not gone. Maybe they never will be. But I've gotten used to ignoring them, and I think that as a result they have kind of given up on me. You think that's what it's like with all our dreams and our nightmares, Martin? You've got to keep feeding them for them to stay alive?" What can we learn from him about the desires of our sinful nature?

2. What advice does Paul offer in Galatians 5:16? Why? (See verse 17.)

3. Answer one of the following:

- On a typical day, what percentage of the time are you winning and what percentage of the time are you losing the battle for control of your desires? If you are a Christian, how is your spiritual battle today different from when you did not know Christ?

- What is the one desire from your sinful nature that most troubles you, and why? What is the way of escape and victory?

4. In *A Beautiful Mind* John Nash also said, "Being part of a community might do me some good. A certain level of attachments to familiar places, familiar people, might help me elbow out these . . . these certain delusions I have." What group can be your "community" to help you "elbow out" your sinful desires? What would you have to do for that to happen? What would the group have to do?

Additional Resources

Hundreds of free articles, videos, and audio messages to help equip you to stand strong in Christ are available at the Web site maninthemirror.org. Helpful video/audio series include:

- "How to Win the Battle for Your Soul"
- "A Man's Guide to Inevitable Events"
- "Biblical Manhood"
- "10 Questions That **Trouble** Every Thinking Man"

PART FOUR

DISCIPLINES RELATED TO A WITNESS FOR GOD

A MAN AND STEWARDSHIP

PREVIEW

In this chapter we will examine stewardship as defined in Scripture. We'll:

- **Recognize that stewardship is a lifestyle of daily choosing to submit to God's agenda, since He owns everything.**
- **Understand our role as caretakers of what is His.**
- **Learn to submit 100 percent of our time, talent, and treasure to God as faithful stewards.**

What was your reaction when you opened to this chapter and saw the topic? My guess is that you had one of two responses:

1. *You groaned*, resigning yourself to sit through another lecture on tithing and giving. You may already be starting to feel very guilty because you are not tithing. The reason for the guilt is that churches all over America plead for men to tithe.

2. *You smiled and rubbed your hands together*, thinking, "I'm already tithing, so I've got this one covered." That's because tithing is often discussed in such a way that when you finally do tithe you think that you have done God a huge favor. You think that you are some sort of spiritual giant!

Guess what. If you already tithe, big deal. If you want to brag about it, you can brag right along with the Pharisees. Any Pharisee can tithe. In fact, this religious group was so scrupulous about money matters that members even measured out the spices in their homes and tithed on their value. But Pharisees tithed without undergoing a change of heart. Jesus said they ignored greater issues like justice, love, mercy, and faithfulness (Matthew 23:23; also Luke 11:42). Jesus said they should have done both—they should have tithed, but they also should have concentrated on the overarching issues that reveal the heart.

Do you think that God wants 10 percent of your money? Forget it. Make no mistake—stewardship is about money. But it's not *just* about money, and certainly not about a measly 10 percent. Ten percent is no big deal. He doesn't want 10 percent of your money. That is so lukewarm. He wants it all.

When you get to tithing, you are only at the starting point of what God wants you to do with your life. In this chapter we will be exploring *stewardship,* not *tithing.* It's not just your money He wants. God wants all of your treasure, all of your time, and all of your talent. He wants it all. God has a purpose for you. He wants to use you to make a difference in the world. Let me tell you, 10 percent isn't going to help. He wants it all. The big idea for this chapter is: A faithful steward devotes 100 percent of his time, talent, and treasure to the glory of God.

What Is Stewardship?

My father was a great man who set a standard for stewardship that will challenge me for the rest of my life. When he died in September of 2002, I became the personal representative for his estate. I took over his checkbook. Because of my responsibility, and also because I was curious, I went through that checkbook. I found no record of any spending that embarrassed me. I found no record that would have embarrassed my father or his Lord.

My dad's example teaches a crucial life lesson. Stewardship isn't just about money. Stewardship is an all-inclusive concept about our faithfulness with all of the time, talent, and treasure God entrusts to us. As Paul wrote in 1 Corinthians 4:2, "Now it is required that those who have been given a trust must prove faithful." Stewardship is how we use all of the resources God gives us.

My grandfather abandoned his family when my dad was only two years old. Grandma suffered a stroke a little later. It affected her speech, and for the rest of her life, she spoke in a slurred way that only a few people could understand. When she walked, she dragged the whole right side of her body. These two events heaped a great deal of stress on the family. Soon they lost their farm in Hayward, Minnesota, and Ida Mae and her four children moved into town to live with two of her sisters.

Those three women raised my father and his three older siblings. My dad's older brother, my uncle Harry, immediately found a job to help support the family. He worked on the bread truck before school, in the butcher shop after school, and at the local filling station on weekends. He was ten years old.

My father began his work life at the age of six. He would get up with his brother at three in the morning, and they would work the bread truck and then deliver newspapers. They had a permanent tardy slip for school.

My dad's legacy will never be measured in terms of money or worldly achievements. My father's mission was to break the cycle. His father abandoned the family, became a criminal, and ended up in prison. By will and determination, despite all the excuses he could have given, my father refused to accept the role of victim. He couldn't change the past, but he worked hard to change the future. He set our whole family on a new course, and I believe it will affect many generations yet to come.

My father's legacy cannot be measured by the standard that most people hold up as the ideal. Most people judge a man's success by how far he goes. My dad's legacy must be judged in terms of how far he came. Was he perfect? No. Was he a faithful steward? Yes.

My father was a faithful steward who focused every day on using 100 percent of his time, talent, and treasure for God's glory. I can't remember a single dishonest act. I can't remember him ever speaking ill of another person, or doing anything that neglected or dishonored my mother. That's quite a legacy. That's what it means to be a faithful steward. It's not about how we handle money or achievements. It's looking honestly at where we came from, appraising our resources—even if they are meager—and then humbly and gratefully using everything entrusted to us to bring glory to God.

Why Is Stewardship Important?

Expressing Our Appreciation to God

People who reduce stewardship to a money issue seem to be under the mistaken impression that God needs 10 percent of their money. In short, why would God be interested in 10 percent when He already owns 100 percent? God doesn't need our money. We need to give money a lot more than God needs to get it.

Frankly, your 10 percent isn't going to be a big bonanza to God. God is not wringing His hands over whether we tithe or not. He has all the resources He needs to accomplish His will. If Jesus was able to take five loaves of bread and two fish from a young boy in the crowd and feed five thousand people until they were full, and had leftovers, my little bit of money is not going to make or break Him.

You see, tithing really isn't about God's need to receive; it's about our need to give. Tithing doesn't earn greater favor with God. Instead, tithing gives us the opportunity to express our appreciation to God for His provision to us, and to participate in building His kingdom. What tithing does is to help us to remember that every good thing comes from Him.

Tithing is not a blessing *for* God, but *from* God. Tithing, instituted by Abraham, is a way of thanking the One who has blessed us: 90 percent for temporal life, 10 percent (or more) for spiritual life. A faithful steward isn't some miserly person who counts out 10 percent to drop in the offering plate Sunday after Sunday. A faithful steward devotes 100 percent of his time, talent, and treasure to God's glory.

Knowing "Everything . . . Is Yours"

We can see in 1 Chronicles 29 how King David "got it"—that he understood stewardship as just described. This passage shows David in his old age nearing the end of his life. He has assembled resources for the temple that his son Solomon will build. People have stepped up to this task, maybe even going beyond tithing. This is one of the last things that we hear from King David:

> Praise be to you, O LORD, God of our father Israel, from everlasting to everlasting. Yours, O LORD, is the greatness and the power and the glory and the majesty and the splendor, for everything in heaven and earth is yours. (1 Chronicles 29:10–11)

Isn't that incredible? David says to God, "Everything in heaven and on earth is yours." Y-O-U-R-S. Some drop the "Y" and make it "ours." But the Bible says "everything" belongs to God. Then David adds,

> Yours, O LORD, is the kingdom; you are exalted as head over all. Wealth and honor come from you; you are the ruler of all things. In your hands are strength and power to exalt and give strength to all. (verses 11–12)

Where do wealth, honor, and strength come from? They come from God. No wonder David went on to exclaim,

> Now, our God, we give you thanks, and praise your glorious name. But who am I, and who are my people, that we should be able to give as generously as this? Everything comes from you, and we have given you only what comes from your hand. (verses 13–14)

We could look at many other passages in God's Word that parallel these ideas, yet this passage aptly summarizes the entire perspective of the Bible about where possessions come from and our stewardship.

Everything we have comes from God, and it belongs to God. If you're a Christian, you don't even own yourself. You've been purchased with the blood of Jesus Christ, through His death. Everything you have is given as a trust with which you must prove faithful. The apostle Paul wrote, "Now it is required that those who have been given a trust must prove faithful" (1 Corinthians 4:2). For the purposes of government and order, you may have deeds or titles to homes and cars. You may have bank accounts and certificates. But if you're a believer, you don't actually own anything—God does.

Before my father passed away, he had papers that said he "owned" a house. But he was really just God's manager. He was managing the use of his car. His wife and children actually belonged to God and were given to my father as a trust. It was his privilege, as a faithful steward, to watch over and enjoy them.

Our understanding of ownership affects our decisions at every level. That is the foundation of biblical stewardship. Any Pharisee can tithe 10 percent, but a faithful steward devotes 100 percent of his time, talent, and treasures to God's glory.

Living Out a Commitment to Stewardship

The Call to Obey

At the most basic level, stewardship requires obedience to God's Word. Years ago in our culture, the word *obey* had a positive connotation. Even today, other cultures value an attitude that conforms to group norms. In our contemporary American culture, though, obedience seems to suggest weakness and subservience.

My generation destroyed the attraction to obedience with our "down with the establishment" mantra. People talk about the Generation Xers starting the postmodern movement, with its resistance to authority. But in reality, my generation started that slide. Baby boomers were the first contemporary generation to attack en masse the ideal of obedience and submission to authority.

Obeying Because We Love Him

Yet God requires that we surrender control to Him—control of our material possessions, our time, our destinies, our families, ourselves. He's saying, "If I can't have it all, I don't want any of it. If I can't have you, I don't want your stuff." He requires faithfulness and daily submission to His agenda. We can only accomplish that as we obey His Word.

That might sound oppressive, yet His Word assures us that it isn't. The apostle John wrote, "This is love for God: to obey his commands. *And his commands are not burdensome,* for everyone born of God overcomes the world" (1 John 5:3–4, emphasis added). Our obedience is not oppressive, because it proceeds from our love for God, and it is birthed by our freedom in Jesus. Through Christ we can be released from whatever holds us in bondage. We have been set free to obey God's Word rather than remain a prisoner to "free will." Free will isn't all it's cracked up to be.

The apostle Paul reminds us that holding fast to our own "free will" really just enslaves us in another way. "Don't you know," he asks, "that when you offer yourselves to someone to obey him as slaves, you are slaves to the one whom you obey—whether you are slaves to sin, which leads to death, or to obedience, which leads to righteousness?" (Romans 6:16). We all serve something. Biblical stewardship means that we choose to serve God.

Suggestions for Pursuing the Discipline of Stewardship

If we agree that stewardship begins by obeying God's Word, the pursuit of this discipline presupposes that you are reading and studying the Bible. Let's do a quick study to see what the Bible says about stewardship.

1. Don't get engrossed with your possessions.

We'll start with 1 Corinthians 7:30–31, which gives significant advice about how to handle possessions. In context, the passage suggests that our time on this earth is short. We should live with that knowledge, so that "those who buy something" will treat it "as if it were not theirs to keep; those who use the things of the world, as if not engrossed in them. For this world in its present form is passing away." Eternal perspective causes us to not hold on too tightly to our possessions.

2. Take care of the possessions you do have.

But other Scriptures indicate that we shouldn't be inattentive to the material goods that God entrusts to us. We aren't called to withdraw from the world, assuming that God will take care of us without our planning or preparation. Scripture calls for a balanced approach on stewardship—accepting that God owns everything but that He entrusts the care of His possessions to us. Proverbs 12:27, for instance, tells us, "The diligent man prizes his possessions." That means if God enables you to own a car, you wash it and you get the oil changed. You take care of it.

3. Provide for the future.

Proverbs 21:20 says, "In the house of the wise are stores of choice food and oil." This verse instructs the wise steward to plan for his financial future. No one else can (or should) take care of you financially. You have to take responsibility for your own retirement, early death, or disability (temporary or permanent). Proverbs 27:23–24 describes the process that encourages that. It says, "Be sure you know the condition of your flocks, give careful attention to your herds; for riches do not endure forever, and a crown is not secure for all generations." Basically, this passage says, "Pay attention to what's going on with your assets, because there's no guarantee that they'll be there forever."

4. Give 10 percent of your income to the work of the church.

I like to think of 10 percent as a tax. It comes right off the top, even before paying the IRS. If the income is from a transaction, I deduct the expenses before calculating the tithe. If you are an independent salesman or business owner, by all means deduct your business expenses, then tithe on your income.

Don't tithe on your income after taxes. If you made $50,000 and paid $10,000 in taxes, consider tithing on the whole $50,000. That's how I do it. If you tithe on the $40,000, you save $1,000, but do your really?

Once you tithe, you don't have to feel guilty for not giving more, and don't let anyone tell you different. However, that doesn't mean you can't give more, and I encourage you to do so. Some Christians believe the entire 10 percent tithe should go to your local church. Others believe some of the 10 percent can be given to Christian ministries. The most conservative view, of course, is to give it all to your church. This is a matter of conscience for you. Have a preference to give to your church, but also feel the freedom to support ministries that work to assist the church. Giving to charitable organizations without a Christian mission doesn't qualify toward the 10 percent.

5. Give above a tithe as God blesses and as you feel led.

The reason I like to think of the tithe as a tax is that once it's paid, my duty is complete. I don't have to feel guilty about not giving more. Quite the opposite, I feel great for giving 10 percent! However, occasionally my wife and I feel led to do something extra. It's not required, but we do it because we can. We do it out of the overflow of gratitude for how God is blessing us at the time. Or sometimes we have given sacrificially out of great need. Either way, remember that it's not required, and it doesn't make God like you any more than He already does.

6. Steward your own private life.

If you hit the wall, we are all going to feel sorry for you, but none of us will feel as if it's our fault. Every man has to take responsibility for his own life. Pay attention to (steward) these five areas, which no one else will look after for you:

- your relationship with God,
- your personal finances,
- your health,
- your relationship with your wife (if applicable), and
- your relationships with your children (if applicable).

Several years ago a friend told me he was working seventy hours a week. We talked about cutting back. He didn't. Several years later, he lost his position as a high-level executive. We talked again and I suggested, "This is God's grace to keep you from destroying yourself. Don't be down about it. Instead, praise God for sparing you, and use this as an opportunity to recalibrate your life to a biblical rhythm." God loves men too much to sit back and watch them slam into a wall at 120 miles an hour.

7. Steward your family.

This is so important it deserves a special mention. When God gives us the gift of a wife and maybe even children, He is giving us a sacred trust for which we are responsible. As mentioned already, a steward devotes 100 percent of his time, talent, and treasure to the glory of God. After God, our family deserves our time the most.

How do we steward our family time? Set your work hours and don't deviate. Personally, my cutoff has always been six o'clock. I work like a dog until six o'clock, and then I quit. No matter what's going on, I don't work nights, and I don't work weekends. When I started to travel and speak, we had a family meeting and decided to limit my travel to five nights a month maximum. Were there exceptions? No, because my family has always been a higher priority to me than work. I may have some flexibility that you don't. But maybe you have more flexibility than you think. It never hurts to ask.

A lot of men will compartmentalize their families while at work, but then come home and not compartmentalize their work. That's poor stewardship! Men, if you don't have enough time for your families, you can be 100 percent certain that you are not following God's will for your life.

I used to have a ten-minute drive home from work. I would allow my mind to decompress and think about work until I got to a small bridge on Howell Branch Road. That bridge was about three minutes from the house. Then I would take all of the papers, figuratively, and I'd put them into an imaginary briefcase, shut it, throw it over the wall and, in my mind, watch it splash into the creek. I did that to clear my mind so that by the time I got home I was ready to re-engage my family. Actually, what I did first was give myself fifteen minutes to wash my face, put on some jeans, and then ask Patsy how she was doing.

From that moment on, I basically gave myself to my children. There were endless repetitions of Chutes and Ladders, mind-numbing sets of Candy Land—both of which require the IQ of a goldfish. I hated those games for the same reason my children loved them. That's because no matter how competitively you play, the other player is still going to win half the games.

Stewardship is a challenging discipline because it affects every aspect of life. Yet a faithful steward is nothing more than a man who has surrendered his agenda to God, accepting and living in submission to His plan. That sounds pretty much like the definition of a Christian. So stewardship is more than an "option" on a long menu. It's not a take-it-or-leave-it thing. It's part of the deal. Stewardship is the inevitable lifestyle of an authentic Christian man. That's why one of my credos is: No agenda but God; no agenda but God's.

Father, from the very beginning of time, our unwillingness to accept that You are God, and we are Your servants, has pulled us away from You. We have been unwilling to submit to Your agenda and to obey Your directives. We have seen stewardship as a side issue related only to our financial decisions. Remind us that stewardship is a lifestyle decision to submit to You as a servant would to his master. May we want to leave a legacy of faithfulness. I don't want You to be embarrassed by what is in my checkbook or on my calendar. I want to invest myself in Your purposes and plans. I want to be a good steward of the resources You've given me. But I know I can only do that as You give wisdom and strength. I'm asking for Your help. In Jesus' name. Amen.

A Review of the Big Ideas

🔥 A faithful steward devotes 100 percent of his time, talent, and treasure to the glory of God.

🔥 Tithing, instituted by Abraham, is a way of blessing the One who has blessed us.

🔥 Don't get engrossed with your possessions.

🔥 Take care of the possessions you do have.

🔥 Provide for the future.

🔥 Give above a tithe (10 percent) as God blesses and you feel led.

🔥 Steward yourself and your family.

🔥 Stewardship is the inevitable lifestyle of an authentic Christian man.

Discussion Questions

1. Why is "discipline" required to be a good steward?

2. Look up these two passages and decide if the primary character was a good steward or a bad steward. Explain why.

Matthew 19:16–24

Luke 21:1–4

3. What is the main point of application for you from 1 Chronicles 29:10–19?

From 1 Corinthians 4:2?

4. Answer one of the following:

• Have you been a good steward of your time? Explain your answer.

• Have you been a good steward of your talent? Explain.

• Have you been a good steward of your treasure? Explain.

• Which of the following words best describes your stewardship, and why? Engrossed, preoccupied, presumption, inattention, engaged, or faithful.

5. What would you like to do differently as a result of this chapter?

Additional Resources

In my book *Ten Secrets for the Man in the Mirror*, there's a chapter entitled "Do What You Don't Want to Do and Become What You Want to Be," which covers other topics related to the topic of *stewardship*.

11

A MAN AND SERVICE

PREVIEW

In this chapter, we will discuss the spiritual discipline of service. We'll:

- **Examine how a service-oriented lifestyle runs counter to our natural desires and to our culture.**
- **Discuss godly motivations for service.**
- **List some ways that service can become part of our daily lives.**

From a practical standpoint, the self-focused lifestyle simply doesn't work. It won't make you happy. In fact, it will make you miserable. But you probably already know that. Thousands of years ago, Solomon also found this to be true. He pursued every possible earthly avenue to find happiness: scientific studies, musical achievements, literary accomplishments, and education. He poured himself into his work, amassing a huge fortune, which he spent on great social projects, public works, and real estate developments.

Solomon was the chief executive officer of the world's largest conglomerate, the president of his country, the commander in chief, number one on the *Forbes* list of billionaires, the greatest patron of the arts, the Poet Laureate of his nation, a Nobel prize–winning scientist, a developer whose buildings would have trumped Trump, and the owner of a fleet of merchant ships. He was the Teacher of the Year and more famous than Lance Armstrong and the American Idol combined. Here's how he summarized his life:

> I denied myself nothing my eyes desired; I refused my heart no pleasure. My heart took delight in all my work, and this was the reward for all my labor. Yet when I surveyed all that my hands had done and what I had toiled to achieve, everything was meaningless, a chasing after the wind; nothing was gained under the sun. (Ecclesiastes 2:10–11)

And then he added, "So I hated life" (verse 17). So much for the self-focused life! The price of getting what you want is getting what you want.

What Is Service?

A managing partner for one of those firms with a long name who had just finished a service project said, "Pat, I don't know what it is, but I feel happier in my life right now than I have in a long time." That is the essence of service. Service is almost always sacrificial, although we will often feel as if we gain more than we give. Like stewardship, it involves submission to God's agenda. It means focusing on someone other than myself.

As servants, we are responsible to help anyone whose need we see and whose need we are in a position to meet. You and I are *not* responsible, however, for the needs we don't know about, or do know about but cannot—or should not—meet. For example, to skip your children's soccer games to spend every Saturday helping widows with home repairs just doesn't sound right.

Jesus does not want us to feel guilty about what we couldn't do, or forget (or devalue) what we were able to do. The Devil, however, wants nothing more. The Devil wants to take our good deeds and convince us that they're never enough: "You could have done more. You should have done more. What about _____? Why didn't you help _____? You have left something undone."

Developing the Mind-Set of a Servant

As with all the disciplines, we're not trying to develop a service mentality simply because we want to get God's attention or improve our spiritual scorecard. Instead, service spills out of a maturing relationship with Jesus Christ. Here's how it works. Early in your spiritual journey, you didn't have enough Jesus for yourself, much less any left over to give away to others. You did your good deeds as duty. However, over time you began to fill up in your personal relationship with Jesus. You began to plumb the depths of His holiness, mercy, love, and grace. You were awestruck by His power, greatness, and majesty. You were humbled by how you had underestimated the work of Jesus. And you grew.

At a point, you realized you finally did have enough Jesus for yourself. You felt filled up in your relationship with Him. That spurred you on to new growth. Another couple of years passed, and one day you realized that you were spilling over with Jesus. Not only did you have enough Jesus for yourself; you had some left over to give away to others as well.

In fact, you were so filled to overflowing that you felt as if you would burst unless you could give some of Him away. That's how a servant is supposed to feel—as if he can no longer be happy unless he does something to serve. Anything less will represent a failure.

Maybe you are there, maybe not. Service is one of the latter disciplines. If you cannot serve out of overflowing gratitude, then don't. Don't pretend to have taken hold of that to which you still aspire. Instead, pursue Christ and let Him continue to sort you, fill you, make you, shape you. When the time is right, you will know what to do.

Obviously, if a man "never" feels compelled to serve, he is either (1) not growing as a disciple or (2) not in Christ.

Jesus: Our Example for Service

Matthew 20 includes an interesting story about the disciples James and John. It records that their mother came to Jesus and requested that her sons be given the honor of sitting at His right and left in His kingdom. Jesus said to them, "You don't know what you are asking. . . . Can you drink the cup I am going to drink? . . . You will indeed drink from my cup, but to sit at my right or left is not for me to grant. These places belong to those for whom they have been prepared by my Father" (see Matthew 20:22–23).

Now put yourself in the place of the other ten disciples. How would you react if you heard that two of your group had tried to elevate themselves above you? You can probably guess that the other disciples were indignant.

Jesus replied, "The rulers of the Gentiles lord it over them, and their high officials exercise authority over them. Not so with you. Instead *whoever wants to become great among you must be your servant, and whoever wants to be first must be your slave—just as the Son of Man did not come to be served but to serve, and to give his life as a ransom for many*" (Matthew 20:25–28, emphasis added).

And He didn't just say it—He did it. And He didn't just do it—He said, "If you want to be great, you do this too." Jesus inverted the world order. In His economy, we achieve greatness through service—by denying ourselves, taking up our crosses, and following His example.

What Did Jesus Do?

A servant is someone who goes where Jesus would go to do what Jesus would do. So if we want to follow His example, we need to know where He would go and what He would do. In John 13, we see Jesus celebrating the Passover with His disciples. This passage says that, as the evening meal was being served, Jesus took off His outer garments. He wrapped a towel around His waist, poured water into a basin, and began washing His disciples' feet.

When he had finished washing their feet, he put on his clothes and went back to his place. "Do you understand what I have done for you?" he asked them. "You call me 'Teacher' and 'Lord,' and rightly so, for that is what I am. Now that I, your Lord and Teacher, have washed your feet, you also should wash one another's feet. *I have set you an example that you should do as I have done for you.* I tell you the truth, no servant is greater than his master, nor is a messenger greater than the one who sent him. Now that you know these things, you will be blessed if you do them." (John 13:12–17, emphasis added)

Of course, Jesus isn't limiting service to washing each other's feet or, for that matter, suggesting that washing feet is what we do. In fact, our service will undoubtedly not be washing feet, but it may be enabling someone to buy shoes, the shoes that will cover their feet. It's the attitude that Jesus is going for here. Instead of waiting to be served, we will choose to take the initiative and serve others.

What Can We Do to Imitate Jesus?

In his book *Celebration of Discipline*, Richard Foster comments on this text from John 13, relating it to the discipline of service. He writes:

> As the cross is the sign of submission, so the towel is the sign of service. Most of us know that we will never be the greatest, just don't let us be the least, right?
>
> Then Jesus took a towel and a basin and redefined greatness.
>
> In some ways we would prefer Jesus' call to deny Father and Mother, houses, and land for the sake of the gospel than his word to wash feet. Radical self-denial gives the feel of adventure. If we have the chance to forsake all then we have the chance to glorious martyrdom. But in service we must experience the many little deaths of going beyond ourselves. Service banishes us to the mundane, the ordinary, the trivial.[1]

We can all agree that living out a life of service is not easy. Yet some people seem to flow more naturally in this area than others. Some men are highly motivated to serve, while others are lukewarm. Certainly part of the difference lies in spiritual gifting, but it also lies in our motivations. The John 13 passage that describes Jesus washing the feet of the disciples also outlines His motivations.

This passage tells us, "Jesus knew that the Father had put all things under his power, and that he had come from God and was returning to God; *so* he got up from the meal" and served (John 13:3–4, emphasis added). Jesus understood His true identity. Because He knew His true identity— who He was and where He was going—He was free to serve. Similarly, our ability to choose a lifestyle of service will flow from understanding who we are and where we are going, because of our relationship with Christ.

Like Isaiah, every man who knows Christ has encountered the living God. Eventually, every true believer hears some form of the words Isaiah heard: "Who will go? Whom shall I send?" When we have settled with the issue of who we are and who He is, our natural response will be like Isaiah's: "Here I am. Send me!" (Isaiah 6:8).

The motivation to follow Jesus' example comes from repeatedly bringing ourselves into the real presence of this holy God. Eventually, our gratitude for His favor will overwhelm us with a desire to serve. So if you don't feel the desire to serve God, don't waste your time doing something you don't want to do. But do put yourself in God's presence. Through Bible study, prayer, meditation, and worship, search the depths of His holiness, His righteousness, His omnipotence, His benevolence, His grace, and His mercy. Seek the King of Kings and Lord of Lords, the Alpha and Omega, the Transcendent God, the Imminent Christ. Bring yourself to Jesus, and in due time you will find yourself motivated to serve.

Suggestions for Pursuing the Discipline of Service

Suggestions from the apostle Peter

Because service breaks out wherever neighbor-love sees a need, its expressions are as boundless as our imaginations. Peter's first epistle tells us, "Above all, love each other deeply, because love covers over a multitude of sins" (1 Peter 4;8). Then Peter gives these suggestions:

> Offer hospitality to one another without grumbling. Each one should use whatever gift he has received to serve others, faithfully administering God's grace in its various forms. If anyone speaks, he should do it as one speaking the very words of God. If anyone serves, he should do it with the strength God provides, so that in all things God may be praised through Jesus Christ." (1 Peter 4:9–11)

Donald Whitney, author of *Spiritual Disciplines for the Christian Life*, summarizes the contemporary expression of that passage like this:

> The ministry of serving may be as public as preaching or teaching, but more often it will be as sequestered as nursery duty. It may be as visible as singing a solo, but usually it will be as unnoticed as operating the sound equipment to amplify the solo. Serving may be as appreciated as a good testimony in a worship service, but typically it is as thankless as washing dishes after a church social. Most service, even that which seems the most glamorous, is like an iceberg. Only the eye of God ever sees the larger, hidden part of it.[2]

Beyond the church walls, serving could be taking a shift for a coworker so he can visit a gravely ill grandparent, running an errand for someone who gets paid to run errands for you, taking meals to needy families (great to do with your children), providing transportation for someone whose car breaks down, feeding pets and watering plants for vacationing neighbors, and hardest of all, having a servant's heart in the home. Serving is as commonplace as the practical needs it seeks to meet, which is why it has to be a discipline. That's why it has to be a cultivated habit.

The Warrior and the Cupbearer

Men want to make a difference. This truth is highlighted in a poignant scene from the movie *Black Hawk Down*. A soldier says, "You really believe in this mission down to your very bones, don't you, Sergeant?"

The sergeant replies, "These people don't have jobs, no food, no education, no future. I figure we have two things we can do: We can help, or we can sit back and watch the country destroy itself on CNN. I was trained to fight, how about you? I was trained to make a difference."

And then there's the approach of Christian author Gary Smalley. Each day when he awakens he takes his figurative empty cup, gets in line, and goes to meet with Jesus. Then during the day he empties out his cup serving others. The next day, he gets up, takes his empty cup, once again stands in line, and starts all over again.

Both warrior and cupbearer are powerful metaphors for how we can serve God. Whether God leads you to fight for your country or humbly serve others, one of the greatest proofs that you are a disciple is that you bear much fruit. Christ put it this way: "This is to my Father's glory, that you bear much fruit, showing yourselves to be my disciples" (John 15:8).

Father, thank You for the dedicated men who are reading this book because they want to learn how to know You better and love You more. Thank You for helping us take an unusual look at the usual. Thank You for reminding us that Your kingdom is upside down to worldly values. Lord, help us to practice a discipline of service in our own lives. Show us places that we have been overlooking and show us additional opportunities. Help us to bear much fruit. We ask this in the name of Jesus. Amen.

A Review of the Big Ideas

❧ As servants, we are responsible to help anyone whose need we see and whose need we are in a position to meet.

❧ That's how a servant is supposed to feel—as if he can no longer be happy unless he does something to serve.

❧ A servant is someone who goes where Jesus would go to do what Jesus would do.

❧ When we have settled the issue of who we are and who He is, our natural response will be like Isaiah's: "Here I am. Send me!"

❧ Bring yourself to Jesus, and in due time you will find yourself motivated to serve.

❧ Because service breaks out wherever neighbor-love sees a need, its expressions are as boundless as our imaginations.

Discussion Questions

1. In your own words, explain why the biblical pursuit of service is not an effort to win God's favor by doing "good deeds."

2. Describe a man whom you know who is highly motivated to serve others. What do you think motivates him?

3. In light of what you've learned in this chapter, especially through discussions of John 13 and Isaiah 6, look up these verses and explain how they provide motivation for service:

Ephesians 2:10

John 15:8

Philippians 2:5–11

James 1:27

James 2:14–17

4. How are you already serving Christ? How much do you have the desire to serve Him more? What will you do next?

Additional Resources

Spiritual Disciplines for the Christian Life, by Donald S. Whitney

12

A MAN AND EVANGELISM

PREVIEW

In this chapter, we will discuss the spiritual discipline of evangelism. We'll:

- **Examine what God sees when He looks at men and women.**

- **Take inventory of the things that make men open to a reasonable explanation of Christianity.**

- **Outline the description of Christianity offered by the apostle Paul.**

- **List some ways to effectively pursue evangelism as a discipline.**

You may be somewhat surprised that I've included evangelism as one of the spiritual disciplines. People have said to me, "Pat, you have the gift of evangelism." I don't. It's true that I do a lot of evangelism, but I do it as an act of discipline. Evangelism is not my natural interest, nor my spiritual gifting. I do it because of the following declaration by Jesus, our Master: "You will receive power when the Holy Spirit comes on you; and you will be my witnesses in Jerusalem, and in all Judea and Samaria, and to the ends of the earth" (Acts 1:7–8).

Clearly from this verse, part of what it means to be a disciple is to be a witness—either by gifting or by discipline. So I look at this verse and say to myself, "I am willing to substitute discipline for a lack of natural interest." I do this for Jesus. I also do it for the men.

Cosmic Loneliness

John Heisman, the Georgia Tech coach for whom the Heisman Trophy is named, was one tough guy. Football in hand, he once told his team, "Gentlemen, it would be better to have died as a small child than to fumble this football." Now that's tough!

We all know men just like that—tougher than nails and harder than granite. They seem impenetrable. Yet we also know that each of these men need—desperately need—Jesus Christ, even if he doesn't know it. Instead, they worship artificial substitutes—little "christs." But even tough guys like John Heisman, after giving twenty, thirty, or even forty years to a particular philosophy of life, come to see that their worldview leaves them feeling empty.

Every person who does not know Christ has made someone or something into a substitute for Christ—it is the need to worship gone awry. That's because every one of us wants to satisfy the deep longing of the human heart for true meaning, substance, purpose, and love. Regrettably, apart from Christ, every such quest comes to nothing. Eventually, those little christs disappoint, often at the worst possible moment, and a cosmic loneliness spreads across a man's soul, leaving a dark stain. They find themselves not only alone in the world (and that's bad enough), but alone in the universe. They are cosmic wanderers whose souls can find no rest.

I once saw a poster hanging on a high school wall that said, "Either we are alone in the universe or we are not. Both ideas are overwhelming." It is a scary feeling. And it will be good if you or I are nearby on that day when the dread of cosmic loneliness catches up with him.

How God Sees People

Now let me tell you about another man—a man for whom I've prayed for two decades. He makes John Heisman look like a wimp. This guy is the most stubborn, proud person I know. Yet to my astonishment, every single area of his life is working for him. I'm sure you know people like that, and you may have given up on them, deeming them "unsaveable." But we cannot succumb to see people the way they are; we must see them the way God sees them.

We get a glimpse of God's attitude in Matthew 9:36. The previous verses tell us that Jesus had been out mingling with people. He was teaching, preaching, and healing. Because all of us are sinners, we could easily understand if verse 36 said, "When he saw the crowds, he was sickened by their depravity." Instead, it says, "When he saw the crowds, *he had compassion on them, because they were harassed and helpless, like sheep without a shepherd*" (emphasis added). That is the attitude of Christ, and that is exactly the way He wants us to see people too.

If we see men in any way other than how God sees them, we may miss our moment to help them. The Bible says, "God our Savior . . . wants all men to be saved and come to a knowledge of [His] truth" (1 Timothy 2:3–4). Salvation comes as a universal invitation. That doesn't mean everyone will accept it. It does mean, however, that God's deep desire is for every single person to be saved. The disciple Peter put it like this: "[God] is patient with you, not wanting anyone to perish, but everyone to come to repentance" (2 Peter 3:9). The Lord Himself says, "I take no pleasure in the death of anyone" (Ezekiel 18:32). If this is how God sees people, why should we see any different?

What Is Evangelism?

Here is a simple definition for *evangelism*: Evangelism is taking someone as far as he or she wants to go with Jesus. Evangelism is not:

- Tricking or terrifying or shaming someone into receiving Christ
- A single strategy, method, or program (though these can be good)
- A contest in which you win if the person becomes a Christian and you lose if they don't
- Only successful if you "close the deal"

Under the proposed definition, evangelism is:

- Centered around the person of Jesus and His offer of salvation

- Low pressure, because you only need to take the person as far as he wants to go

- Sometimes brings in a harvest, but more often sows seeds

- Not a thing that must produce immediate results

When we present the gospel, we must understand that God's timing is mysterious and cannot be orchestrated. Further, we must realize that God is more interested in someone's salvation than we will ever be, so we can relax.

In this information age, everyone is at least somewhat aware of Christianity—usually through caricatures of phonies and wimps. In most cases, however, people who reject Christianity have never properly understood it. Evangelism is the process by which we help unbelieving men and women see God as He is and respond to Him by accepting His offer of salvation through the sacrificial death of His Son, through the working of the Holy Spirit. The task of evangelism is to take away people's misunderstandings so that, if they do reject Christianity, they are at least rejecting what it really is.

When Are Men Open to Evangelism?

How do such men—misty, lonely, harassed, and helpless—become open to the gospel of Jesus Christ? I believe it happens when, through recognizing life's futility, they seek to overcome their cosmic loneliness. This can happen in several ways.

1. *A man can become overwhelmed with eternity*. At some point, every man looks at the host of stars in the night sky and asks, "Where is the edge of eternity? Where does infinity begin? Does it end where it begins, or vice versa?" We all have experiences that overwhelm us as we contemplate our place in the universe. And we can't help but experience that cosmic loneliness when we consider the vastness of eternity without a personal God.

2. *A man can be pierced by the brevity of life.* It usually happens suddenly, when we see a young child snatched away by disease or mortal injury. Or when we meet a middle-aged man who has lost almost all of his lung capacity and must live with unexpected limitations. In those circumstances, we come face-to-face with mortality. We recognize that our whole existence, with all its problems and relationships and disappointments and failures and successes, fits within a pinch of eternity. A brief interlude . . . and it's gone. That process can move a man to face his cosmic loneliness.

3. *A man can be overwhelmed with moral guilt.* We all do bad, sinful things. Even the worst of sinners, by God's grace, through the Holy Spirit, may experience a sense of godly sorrow for attitudes and actions that have displeased God. That guilt can lead to repentance as a man deals with the accompanying sense of cosmic loneliness, asking himself, "What do I do with this guilt? How do I unburden myself? How do I take care of this?"

4. *A man can fear death.* He might get an unexpectedly negative diagnosis from the doctor. He might be driving and just miss being in a serious accident. He might take on a new career that includes physical risk. What man, contemplating his own death, would intentionally choose to go alone across the precipice from this life to the next, and not feel the weight of cosmic loneliness?

5. *A man may long for transcendence.* All men long to experience ultimate reality—something that goes beyond the mere tangible existence of this life. If we don't know Christ as the source of everything we see, we try to fill that void in many different ways. Some men go to bars, some chase women, some try to accumulate achievements, others accumulate money. None of these aspirations will fill the void created by cosmic loneliness. The one true solution is a relationship with God. The pursuit of substitutes will always, thanks to the grace of God, end in futility.

You and I are called to take God's message of love and redemption to these men—either by gifting or as an act of discipline. There are 113 million men in the United States fifteen years of age and older, and 69 million of them do not profess to be born again.

Many of these men—men in your neighborhood, your workplace, your gym—will someday soon be overwhelmed by eternity, be pierced by the brevity of life, be overwhelmed by moral guilt, fear death, or long for transcendence. At that moment when it dawns on a man that he is not only alone in the world, but alone everywhere, and he reaches out, if we have been faithful to the discipline of evangelism, he will know to whom he can reach, and we will be there for him. We prepare for that day by building relationships with men, and by seeing men the way God sees them—harassed and helpless, like sheep without a shepherd.

Living Out the Discipline of Evangelism

Let's go back to that passage in Matthew 9. After Jesus reflected on the spiritual state of the people, He told His disciples, "The harvest is plentiful, but the workers are few. Ask the Lord of the harvest, therefore, to send out workers into his harvest field" (verses 37–38).

There is no shortage of believers, but there is a shortage of workers. As I said, 113 million men live right here in the United States. More than half of them are spiritual zombies. Every other man you meet today is a dead man walking, and many would be open to the gospel if someone would be disciplined enough to tell them. They are walking around either pretending they have it all together, or pretending they don't care at all. In either case, they are pretending.

Why are most Christians not responding to these needy men? Because once we see men as God sees them, we must still find a source of motivation to fuel our discipline. We need look no further than our brother in the battle, the apostle Paul. "But whatever was to my profit I now consider loss for the sake of Christ. What is more, I consider everything a loss compared with the surpassing greatness of knowing Christ Jesus my Lord, for whose sake I have lost all things. I consider them rubbish, that I may gain Christ" (Philippians 3:7–8).

In Romans 1:16, this same man wrote, "I am not ashamed of the gospel, because it is the power of God for the salvation for everyone who believes." In 1 Corinthians 2:2 he explained, "I resolved to know nothing while I was with you except Jesus Christ and him crucified." And in 1 Corinthians 9:16 Paul noted, "When I preach the gospel, I cannot boast, for I am compelled to preach. Woe to me if I do not preach the gospel!"

What compelled Paul to discipline himself to this heavy commitment to evangelism? What beliefs fostered these statements? If we could believe what Paul believed, and see what God sees, then to us evangelism would be everything, and everything would be evangelism! So let's look at what Paul knew.

- *He understood the enormity of eternity*. Paul believed in an actual heaven, an actual hell, and an actual salvation.

- *He understood that all men need a Savior*. This is Christianity's fundamental teaching. We all are sinful people who need a Savior.

- *He understood that Jesus is the only Savior*. In John 14:6, Jesus told His disciples, "I am the way and the truth and the life. No one comes to the Father except through me." He is the exclusive way. Paul knew this, believing that salvation was not a result of personal good behavior, but of repentance and faith in Jesus.

That was why Paul was so committed to evangelism. He believed life's greatest privilege is to be chosen by God to receive salvation. And the second greatest privilege is to help someone else to experience that same salvation.

How to Lead a Man to Christ

Today millions of men in America wake up ready to hear a credible explanation of how Christian faith could change their futile lives. Most of these men will go to bed tonight without getting one. Here are five steps you can take to discipline yourself to be a soul winner:

- *Step One: Pray for men.* Ask God to put "prepared" men on your heart.

- *Step Two: Make an appointment.* Take the men God puts on your heart to breakfast, lunch, or out for a cup of coffee.

- *Step Three: Listen.* Ask a man, "Where are you on your spiritual pilgrimage?" I've only had one man out of thousands I've asked in over thirty years who wasn't interested in talking about it.

- *Step Four: Share your testimony.* Tips for preparing an easy-to-say testimony are included the next section.

- *Step Five: Explain how to receive Christ.* If the person's spiritual condition is not already clear to you, ask, "(Name), has there ever been a time in your life when you have personally put your faith in Christ to forgive your sins and receive the gift of eternal life?"

Two steps need more ink. First, you should be able to give him *the testimony of how you became a Christian.* Second, you should be able to show him *God's plan of salvation in the Bible.*

How to Give Your Testimony

The example of your changed life will (usually) do more to "draw" a man toward Jesus than anything else. My apologetics professor in seminary said, "Despite all the intellectual arguments for the existence of God, still the most powerful argument of all is a changed life." However, it is not enough for men to *see* you are different—they need to know why. For that, you will have to *speak.*

Once you've listened and sense a man knows you are on his side, give him your testimony. Your own story is 100 times more powerful than telling him the "theology" of Christianity alone. Be prepared to do this in not more than ten minutes, but also in three minutes if the time is short. In equal time segments tell him three things:

- *Before:* What was your life like before you embraced Jesus?
  Empty, confused, lonely, disillusioned, futile, lacking significance,

without purpose or meaning, successful but still not happy? As much as possible, relate your story to what you know about his story.

- *How*: How did you come to profess faith in Jesus? Where? Who showed you the way? Why did you respond? Be sure to mention conviction of your sins, hunger for truth, understanding who Christ is, repentance, and faith in Jesus.

- *After*: What has Christ done in your life since? Pick areas that have changed that relate to his struggles.

A Challenge: If you want to get serious about sharing Christ with men (or already are), don't shoot from the hip. Take a couple of hours and write out, time, practice, and memorize a three-minute testimony. Pick words that sparkle and emote. Mark Twain said, "A powerful agent is the right word." And you already know what would happen if Michael Jordan didn't practice.

Next, Explain How to Receive Christ

If it is not already clear to you, ask, "(Name), has there ever been a time in your life when you have personally put your faith in Christ to forgive your sins and receive the gift of eternal life?"

If the person answers yes, ask him to describe it. If he can give a clear testimony, affirm him. If not, proceed as though he answered no.

If no, say, "May I take a few minutes and explain what Christians believe about who Jesus is, why He came, and what believing in Him means?"

Then, read him a gospel tract. Personally, I just read men *The Four Spiritual Laws* tract published by Campus Crusade for Christ. (You can get them at Christian bookstores. Also, most denominations and many other ministries also offer tracts.) That's right. I just read it to the person without embellishment or side comments. In fact, since I've read through it word for word with men so often, sometimes my mind will wander and think about things I need to get done during the day ahead. And it makes no difference. In fact, in one way it is evidence that it is God doing the saving rather than my persuasiveness injected into the equation of trying to lead this man to Christ. It is simply allowing the gospel to be the gospel.

If you prefer to not use a tract, you can look up the following verses and read them together. Make sure he reads the words for himself, whether silently or out loud. *Idea:* Mark Bible pages you want to look up with Post It notes. Number them 1, 2, 3, and so on.

1. Who is Jesus?

- *He is the Savior.* "The woman said, 'I know that Messiah' (called Christ) 'is coming. When he comes, he will explain everything to us.' Then Jesus declared, 'I who speak to you am he'"" (John 4:25–26).

- *He is God.* "The Son is the radiance of God's glory and the exact representation of his being" (Hebrews 1:3). "He is the image of the invisible God" (Colossians 1:15). "For in Christ all the fullness of the Deity lives in bodily form" (Colossians 2:9). Jesus Himself said, "Anyone who has seen me has seen the Father" and "I and the Father are one" (John 14:9; 10:30).

- *He is the only way to the Father.* Jesus said, "I am the way and the truth and the life. No one comes to the Father except through me" (John 14:6).

2. Why did Jesus come?

- *To seek the lost.* Jesus said, "For the Son of Man came to seek and to save what was lost" (Luke 19:10).

- *To save sinners.* "Here is a trustworthy saying that deserves full acceptance: Christ Jesus came into the world to save sinners" (1 Timothy 1:15).

- *To demonstrate God's love.* "You see, at just the right time, when we were still powerless, Christ died for the ungodly. Very rarely will anyone die for a righteous man, though for a good man someone might possibly dare to die. But God demonstrates his own love for us in this: While we were still sinners, Christ died for us" (Romans 5:6–8).

- *To atone for our sins.* "This is how God showed his love among us: He sent his one and only Son into the world that we might live through him. This is love: not that we loved God, but that he loved us and sent his Son as an atoning sacrifice for our sins" (1 John 4:9–10).

- *To become the source of eternal salvation.* "Although he was a son, he learned obedience from what he suffered and, once made perfect, he became the source of eternal salvation for all who obey him" (Hebrews 5:8–9).

3. What does Jesus do for those who receive Him as Savior?

- *Gives eternal life.* "For God so loved the world that he gave his one and only Son, that whoever believes in him shall not perish but have eternal life," Jesus told Nicodemus, a religious leader (John 3:16). Later He told Martha, whose brother, Lazarus, had died, "I am the resurrection and the life. He who believes in me will live, even though he dies; and whoever lives and believes in me will never die" (John 11:25). Romans 6:23 says, "For the wages of sin is death, but the gift of God is eternal life in Christ Jesus our Lord."

- *Forgives sins.* "If we claim to be without sin, we deceive ourselves and the truth is not in us. If we confess our sins, he is faithful and just and will forgive us our sins and purify us from all unrighteousness" (1 John 1:8–9).

- *Grants the name and privileges of "children of God."* "Yet to all who received him, to those who believed in his name, he gave the right to become children of God" (John 1:12).

4. How do you become a follower of Jesus?

- *We become Christians through repentance and faith.* "For it is by grace you have been saved, through faith—and this not from yourselves, it is the gift of God—not by works, so that no one can boast." (Ephesians 2:8–9).

  Tell your man, "Nothing we do can ever make us good enough for God to love us. Instead, He loves us, because He made us, and Jesus died for our sins. We become a Christian by confessing that we are sinful and putting faith in Jesus to forgive our sins and by grace give us the gift of eternal life. Prayer is the way we talk to God. Here is a suggested prayer.

"Lord Jesus, I need You in my life. I confess that I am sinful and that I need a Savior. Thank You for dying for my sins. Thank You for offering me the gift of eternal life. By faith I now put my trust in You to forgive my sins and give me the gift of eternal salvation. I invite You to change me and make me the man You want me to be. Amen."

After reading the prayer aloud, ask him if this prayer expresses the desire of his heart. If he says, yes, then ask him to pray it out loud after you one phrase at a time. Congratulate him. Offer to help him grow. Invite him to church. Encourage him to share what he has done with loved ones. See if he would feel comfortable sharing it right away with someone in your presence. Make it a celebratory moment—on earth as it is in heaven.

Letting the Gospel Come Through

When we don't try to "help" God save a man, it lets the gospel come through. Oswald Chambers said it well: "Belief in Jesus is a miracle produced only by the efficacy of Redemption, not by impressiveness of speech, not by wooing and winning, but by the sheer unaided power of God." You don't have to be good; you just have to be available. Just read them the tract or verses. Don't get in the way. The Holy Spirit will do the work.

Let men be amazed by the gospel of Jesus, not you.

It can be nerve-wracking to step out, but there is so much cosmic lone-liness out there. People really want to talk about this. And remember, you don't have to produce any particular result. Here is my advice: Just help a man go as far toward Christ as he wants to go that day. It could be all the way! Or it could be that he just needs someone who can understand his plight. That's the discipline of evangelism—it's just helping people to move as far toward Jesus as they are willing to go.

Heavenly Father, I pray that You would burn this reminder in our hearts. If any of us have wrong attitudes toward people—if we haven't been seeing people as You see them—please give us new eyes. I also pray that You would give us faith to believe and trust in the Scriptures. Help us believe what Paul believed, that we might be motivated to break out of apathy and fear, or whatever hinders us. For all the lost men in our lives, please consume them with a sense of cosmic loneliness, that they might turn to You for salva-tion. Help us to substitute discipline where we lack natural interest. We pray this in the name of Jesus. Amen.

A Review of the Big Ideas

ᵤ If we see men in any way other than how God sees them, we may miss our moment to help them.

ᵤ Evangelism is taking someone as far as he wants to go toward Jesus.

ᵤ The best method of evangelism is the one you will use.

ᵤ Evangelism is the process by which we incrementally help unbelieving men and women see God as He is and respond to Him by accepting His offer of salvation through the sacrificial death of His Son, through the working of the Holy Spirit.

ᵤ The task of evangelism is to take away people's mist so that, if they do reject Christianity, they are at least rejecting what it really is.

ᵤ First, you should be able to give him the testimony of how you became a Christian.

ᵤ Second, you should be able to show him God's plan of salvation in the Bible.

Discussion Questions

1. When are men open to Christ? How sensitive are you to noticing open men?

2. How does God see men according to Matthew 9:36; 1 Timothy 2:4; 2 Peter 3:9; and Ezekiel 18:23, 32? What adjustments do you need to make in your own thinking?

3. How close are you to reflecting in your own life what Paul expressed in Philippians 3:7–11?

4. Based on the Scriptures included in this chapter, what must we believe if we are to make sharing our faith a discipline and a priority?

- About eternity?

- About the need for a Savior?

- About Jesus as the only way of salvation?

- About repentance?

- About faith?

AFTERWORD

Our time together has come to an end, at least for now. But before you move on, I want to once again say that the goal of this book has not been to teach you how to be better. That is not the gospel. The gospel of Jesus Christ is about calling us to daily repentance and faith—not about improving our record by trying harder. So we pursue the spiritual disciplines as a grateful response to God's grace, as a way to cultivate a deeper walk with Christ. We do not perform disciplines to impress God.

Here are the twelve disciplines we've explored all together. I've put in some space for you to jot down a takeaway, big idea, or action item that is most meaningful to you for each of the disciplines. Then I would encourage you to take that action or apply that idea to your life.

< **A Man and Creation** _____

_____

< **A Man and the Bible** _____

_____

< **A Man and Prayer** _____

_____

< **A Man and Worship** _____

_____

< **A Man and the Sabbath** _____

_____

< **A Man and Fellowship** _____

_____

< **A Man and Counsel** _____

_____

< **A Man and Fasting** _____

_____

< **A Man and Spiritual Warfare** _____

_____

< **A Man and Stewardship** _____

_____

< **A Man and Service** _____

_____

< **A Man and Evangelism** _____

_____

May God honor you as you honor Him through these disciplines. I pray that God will give you the desires of your heart.

NOTES

Introduction

1. Patrick Morley, David Delk, and Brett Clemmer, *No Man Left Behind* (Chicago: Moody, 2006), 33.

Chapter 1: A Man and Creation

1. C. S. Lewis, *The Problem of Pain* (New York: Collier, 1962),13–15.
2. Francis A. Schaeffer, *Escape from Reason* (Downers Grove, Ill.: InterVarsity, 1968), 14.
3. Rudolph Otto, *The Idea of the Holy* (London: Oxford Univ. Press, 1923), 12–13.

Chapter 2: A Man and the Bible

1. Peter Cousins, "The Bible Is Different," *Eerdman's Handbook to the Bible,* ed. David Alexander and Pat Alexander (Grand Rapids: Eerdmans: 1973), 33.
2. Josh McDowell, *The New Evidence that Demands a Verdict* (Nashville: Nelson, 1999), 34–38.

Chapter 3: A Man and Prayer

1. C. S. Lewis, *God in the Dock* (Grand Rapids: Eerdmans, 1970), 106–107.
2. Ibid., 107.

3. See Patrick Morley, *Man in the Mirror* (Nashville: Nelson, 1999), chapter 8.

4. John Rossomando, "*Born-Again Christians No More Immune to Divorce Than Others, Says Author,*" CNS News, http://www.cnsnews.com/ViewCulture.asp?/Page-/culture/archive/200201/CUL20020121b.html.

Chapter 4: A Man and Worship

1. J. I. Packer, *A Quest for Godliness* (Wheaton, Ill.: Crossway, 1990), 249.

2. Ibid.

3. Douglas Coupland, *Life After God* (New York: Pocket, 1994), 359.

4. C. S. Lewis, *The Weight of Glory*, "Introduction by Walter Hooper" (New York: Simon & Schuster, 1949), 15–16.

5. Ibid., 16.

6. Richard Baxter, *The Reformed Pastor* (1656; repr., Edinburgh: The Banner of Truth Trust, 1989), 101.

Chapter 6: A Man and Fellowship

1. Robert Coleman, *The Master Plan of Evangelism* (1963; repr. Ventura, Calif.: Regal, 1998), 98.

Chapter 11: A Man and Service

1. Richard J. Foster, *Celebration of Discipline* (New York: Harper & Row, 1988), 126–27.

2. Donald Whitney, *Spiritual Disciplines for the Christian Life* (Colorado Springs: NavPress, 1991)110.

THE KEY TO LASTING CHANGE IN OUR FAMILIES, CHURCHES, AND COMMUNITIES CAN BE FOUND IN DISCIPLING MEN FOR CHRIST.

The team at Man in the Mirror has just completed a milestone project that delivers a proven, step-by-step process for discipling every man in your church. The fruit of thirty years of combined research and experience in over 2,500 churches, *No Man Left Behind* addresses the critical issues related to men's ministry, including:

■ Shifting your paradigm from men's ministry to ministering to all your men
■ Determining the unwritten "man code" your church projects to every guy who walks in the door
■ Ensuring long-term success by recruiting allies who will help you make disciples
■ Meeting the needs of first-time guys and seasoned disciples
■ Giving men a compelling reason to get involved

To download a free chapter, go to: www.maninthemirror.org/NMLB

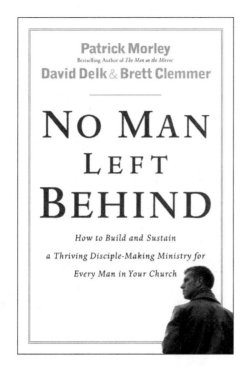

*No Man Left Behind: How to Build and Sustain a Thriving
Disciple-Making Ministry For Every Man in Your Church*
ISBN-10: 0-8024-7549-3; Hardcover; 224 pages
ISBN-13: 978-0-8024-7549-7

Plus, this book is also a training conference available to leaders around
the country! Spend two and a half days with pastors and men's ministry
leaders working together to apply the *No Man Left Behind* model in each
church.

Events are scheduled in Orlando, Los Angeles, Waco, Oklahoma City,
and more, with additional cities being added every week! For a complete
schedule, or to learn how to bring the *No Man Left Behind* conference to
your area, call or visit:

800-929-2536 / www.maninthemirror.org